Pensions and New York City's Fiscal Crisis

Damodar Gujarati

American Enterprise Institute for Public Policy Research
Washington, D.C.

Damodar Gujarati is professor of economics and finance at Baruch College, City University of New York.

Library of Congress Cataloging in Publication Data

Gujarati, Damodar.
  Pensions and New York City's fiscal crisis.

  (AEI studies; 212)
  1. Civil service pensions—New York (City)—
Finance. I. Title. II. Series: American Enterprise
Institute for Public Policy Research. AEI studies; 212.
JS1234.A4   1978   352'.005'5097471   78-11513
ISBN 0-8447-3314-8

AEI Studies 212

Printed in the United States of America

Pensions and New York City's Fiscal Crisis

CONTENTS

CONTENTS

1

New York City's Fiscal Crisis

To appreciate the role of pensions in the New York City fiscal crisis, it is essential to understand the nature of the crisis. In the spring of 1975 the city lacked sufficient funds to meet payrolls and debts that had come due. Whenever this had happened in the past, the city had resorted to short-term (less than a year) borrowing, taking advantage of the unusually liberal borrowing power granted it by the state. Most municipalities are prevented by law or charter from issuing short-term debt to cover current (operating) expenses, and those cities that are allowed to do so must usually pay off such debt during the course of the year. New York City is also required by law to balance its budget every year, but by a variety of financial "gimmicks" it managed to evade the law. The city's delaying tactics included putting day-to-day expense items into the Capital Budget, which is financed entirely by long-term borrowing; postponing to subsequent years payrolls and other expenditures it could not meet; and counting as income for the current fiscal year revenues from the state, federal aid, and taxes that would not materialize until after the current year was actually over.[1]

By the spring of 1975 New York City had piled up a budget deficit exceeding $3 billion, and its short-term borrowing needs exceeded $7 billion. On June 11, 1975, $792 million of the outstanding short-term debt was due to mature, but the city did not have money to pay it off. Moreover, because of the city's frequent borrowing in

---

[1] For example, expenses incurred for manpower training and job placement have been moved since 1966 from the Expense Budget to the Capital Budget. At about the same time, the city started capitalizing long-term leases. The reason for these shifts was to facilitate borrowing money: it is easier to borrow on capital account because of the state control over such borrowings.

the past, major New York City banks and other financial institutions were not willing to lend it any more money. These institutions had in fact given explicit warning to the city in December 1974 when they lent it $600 million at 9.5 percent per year interest—by any measure an astounding rate for tax-free municipal borrowing.

After some temporary rescue operations and in the face of an imminent default on the outstanding short-term loans due on June 11, 1975, the New York state legislature on June 10, 1975, passed the Municipal Assistance Corporation Act and created the Municipal Assistance Corporation (MAC), popularly known as "Big Mac." Big Mac was authorized to issue $3 billion of its own securities (called the "moral obligation" bonds of the state) with maturities of up to fifteen years over the next three months and to turn over the cash to the city. In other words, Big Mac was to do the borrowing for the city, which had lost its credit in the financial markets. In return, Big Mac was to receive revenues from the city sales tax and stock transfer tax to cover the interest costs on the bonds.

In its first month of operation, Big Mac was able to raise $1 billion at a tax-free rate of interest of 9 percent. But it soon became apparent that even at this high rate, Big Mac could not find investors for its additional $2 billion worth of securities. In September 1975 another default seemed imminent. To stave off the default and instill confidence in the investing community, the state legislature passed, on September 9, 1975, the Financial Emergency Act and created the Emergency Financial Control Board (EFCB). The seven-member EFCB was dominated by state appointees and was authorized full control over the financial affairs of the city for the following three years. Its jurisdiction extended not only to the agencies under the direct control of the mayor, but also to the city's semi-independent agencies that provided elementary and secondary education, higher education, and hospital and other services. Indeed, the authority of the EFCB was such that the mayor and the city council were virtually powerless, at least through the emergency.

The EFCB was required to approve a three-year fiscal plan that included four points: transition to a truly balanced budget by fiscal 1978; reduction in short-term city borrowing; removal of expense items from the Capital Budget; and growth in controllable spending (all but welfare, pensions, and debt service) of not more than 2 percent per year. In addition, the EFCB was given five responsibilities: estimating the city's revenues and keeping spending within these limits; reviewing and approving major labor contracts; approving all city borrowing; extending, if necessary, the pay freeze on city employees through fiscal 1977; and disbursing city revenues, but only after it was satisfied that the expenditures were consistent with the three-year fiscal plan.

Pursuant to the legislation, the EFCB developed in October 1975 a complicated three-year financial plan that was designed to balance the city's budget by the fiscal year ending June 30, 1978. The philosophy underlying the plan was that with a balanced budget, the city could return to the credit market on its own after fiscal 1978 to satisfy its future borrowing needs. The plan that finally emerged in December 1975 included these proposals:

- Big Mac securities (long-term) were to be exchanged for the short-term outstanding securities of the city.
- The major New York City banks and the city's major pension funds agreed to purchase additional securities.
- The state was to advance $800 million annually to the city.
- A moratorium on the repayment of principal on outstanding city notes was to be passed.
- The federal government was to provide substantial credit directly to the city.

In December 1975 the federal government agreed to provide the city with $126 million of credit in fiscal 1976 and with up to $2.3 billion for each of the latter two years of the plan. The pension funds and the state fulfilled their obligations under the plan.

The year 1976 was relatively quiet for the city, except that in November the state's highest court, the New York State Court of Appeals, held that the moratorium on repaying city notes was unconstitutional. However, after an initial scare, a plan was developed in March 1977 to repay almost $1 billion in short-term city notes that had been subject to the moratorium. The EFCB and state and local officials then believed that the city would be able to ride out the crisis without additional problems. And as a matter of fact, the fiscal 1978 budget of about $13.9 billion, which was approved by the EFCB, was balanced, at least on paper.

City Revenues and Expenditures

This outline of the events of 1975 raises the gnawing question, How did the Big Apple lurch into virtual bankruptcy? To answer this question, one has to look at the city's revenues and expenditures over the preceding several years (see Table 1).

Although a city the size of New York ought to have reliable

TABLE 1

New York City Expense Budgets, Fiscal Years 1961–1976
(thousands of dollars)

Fiscal Year Ending June 30	Total Revenue	Total Expenses[a]	Revenue − Expense
1961	2,453,636	2,428,223[b]	25,413
1962	2,579,359	2,622,319	−42,960
1963	2,777,232	2,831,887	−54,655
1964	3,124,354	3,128,496	−4,142
1965	3,391,695	3,391,656	39
1966	3,894,035	3,804,360	89,675[c]
1967	4,616,273	4,542,310	73,963
1968	5,272,401	5,321,959	−49,448
1969	6,149,821	6,087,877	61,944
1970	6,590,900	6,722,072	−131,172
1971	7,823,966	7,848,461	−24,495
1972	8,650,718	8,538,808	111,910
1973	9,444,855	9,369,469	75,386
1974	10,138,773	10,249,513	−110,740
1975	11,964,712	12,033,461	−68,749
1976	11,380,802	12,549,071	−1,168,269
Compound annual growth rate (percent)	10.77	11.57	

[a] Excludes pensions and debt service of the sanitation and health department.
[b] Excludes $13.2 million redemption of budget notes.
[c] Includes $69,000,000 received pursuant to Chapters 2 and 3 of the Laws of 1966, of which $63,750,000 is appropriated in the 1966–67 Expense Budget as "special funds."

SOURCE: New York City, *Comptroller's Annual Report*, various issues.

economic statistics readily available, this is often not the case. The city maintains two types of budgets: the Expense Budget and the Capital Budget. The Expense Budget, dealing with current operating expenditures, is prepared at the beginning of the fiscal year and is therefore tentative. The *Comptroller's Annual Report*, which comes out at the end of the fiscal year, purports to update the Expense Budget, taking into account all changes that took place in the fiscal year. Therefore, there is very often a substantial discrepancy between the Expense Budget and the comptroller's report. The various footnotes that go with the report are often unclear, and there is no assurance that all items of expenditure and revenue due in a given fiscal year are in fact attributed to that year.

4

In nine out of the sixteen years reported in Table 1, the city had budget deficits, the highest being about $1.2 billion in fiscal 1976. The cumulative deficits in 1974 and 1975 brought the financial crisis to a head in the spring of 1975,[2] when the city could no longer borrow in the short-term money market. The real gravity of the city's fiscal plight is shown in Table 2, which gives the city's short-term and long-term debt obligations for the period 1961–1975. Since about 1966, when John V. Lindsay became mayor, the Expense Budget was artificially low because of items shifted to the Capital Budget. Needless to say, if such items had been retained in the Expense Budgets, the deficits there would have been much larger.

Table 2 shows the rapid growth of the short-term debt in three ways: absolutely, relative to the long-term debt, and relative to the total debt outstanding. Between 1961 and 1975 short-term debt grew at a compound annual rate of about 18 percent, the most significant growth—about 28 percent—taking place since 1970. If the amount of new short-term debt equals exactly the amount redeemed in a given year, the city has "rolled over" its debt obligations. But in all years shown except 1962, 1966, and 1973, the city more than rolled over its debt; in each other year the city created additional amounts of short-term debt. This was one of the techniques that enabled the city to "balance" its budget year after year. The city had lost sight of the primary purpose of short-term borrowing, namely, to synchronize its expenditures with its revenues over the fiscal year. Short-term debt is not suited to be a permanent and ever-escalating instrument of finance.

As a result of the increasing amount of both short- and long-term debt, the city's debt service cost increased enormously. In fiscal 1961 the debt service charge was $402 million, whereas in fiscal 1975 it was $2.3 billion, an increase of $1.9 billion. This amounts to a compound annual growth rate of about 12 percent.

Causes of the Crisis

The recurrent budget deficits and the attendant borrowing were but symptoms of a deeper malady. The real basis of the crisis was that the city lived beyond its means—year after year its expenditures increased more than its tax revenues. The two expenditure items, besides the debt service cost, that spiraled were the social welfare and labor costs, especially the costs of pensions, fringe benefits, and social security taxes.

---

[2] If the aid received by the city from the federal and state governments had been excluded from the Expense Budget, the deficit would have been much larger.

TABLE 2

NEW YORK CITY SHORT-TERM AND LONG-TERM DEBT, FISCAL YEARS 1961–1975

Fiscal Year Ending June 30	Short-Term Debt Outstanding[a] (thousands of dollars)	Percent Increase over Previous Year	Long-Term Debt Outstanding[b] (thousands of dollars)	Percent Increase over Previous Year	Short-Term Debt as a Percentage of Long-Term Debt	Short-Term Debt as a Percentage of Total Debt
1961	473,924	—	5,715,081	—	8.29	7.66
1962	470,500	−0.72	5,355,000	−6.30	8.79	8.08
1963	627,500	33.37	6,185,000	15.50	10.14	9.21
1964	712,803	13.59	6,337,878	2.47	11.25	10.11
1965	896,007	25.70	6,563,147	3.55	13.65	12.01
1966	695,452	−22.38	7,001,482	6.68	9.93	9.04
1967	859,804	23.63	7,059,085	0.82	12.18	10.86
1968	874,033	1.65	7,043,443	−0.22	12.41	11.04
1969	880,347	0.72	7,122,211	1.22	12.36	11.00
1970	1,443,974	64.02	7,246,836	1.75	19.93	16.61
1971	2,531,717	75.33	7,633,424	5.33	33.17	24.90
1972	2,874,404	13.54	8,404,563	10.10	34.20	25.48
1973	2,761,642	−3.90	9,002,101	7.11	30.68	23.48
1974	3,700,475	33.99	9,808,248	8.96	37.73	27.39
1975	4,884,022	31.98	9,909,784	1.04	49.28	33.01
Compound annual growth rate (percent)	18.13		4.00			

[a] Interest-bearing debt payable within one year from date of issue, such as bond anticipation notes, bank loans, and tax anticipation notes and warrants.

[b] Debt payable more than one year after date of issue.

SOURCE: U.S. Department of Commerce, Bureau of the Census, *City Government Finances*, various issues.

TABLE 3

NEW YORK CITY EXPENDITURES ON SOCIAL WELFARE, FISCAL YEARS 1961–1976

Fiscal Year Ending June 30	Total Expenditure (thousands of dollars)	Expenditure on Social Welfare (thousands of dollars)	Social Welfare Expenditure as a Percentage of Total
1961	2,428,223	353,071	14.54
1962	2,622,319	384,924	14.68
1963	2,831,887	414,215	14.63
1964	3,128,496	487,262	15.58
1965	3,391,656	563,609	16.62
1966	3,804,366	710,263	18.67
1967	4,542,310	943,066[a]	20.76
1968	5,321,959	1,399,146[a]	26.29
1969	6,087,877	1,790,424	29.41
1970	6,722,072	1,885,726	28.05
1971	7,848,461	2,313,944	29.48
1972	8,538,808	2,589,170	30.32
1973	9,369,469	2,784,247	29.72
1974	10,249,513	2,962,878	28.91
1975	12,033,461	3,431,925	28.52
1976	12,549,071	3,691,094	29.41
Compound annual growth rate (percent)	11.57	16.94	

[a] Excludes pensions and debt service.
SOURCE: New York City, *Comptroller's Annual Report*, various issues.

Social Welfare Costs. Expenditures on social welfare, especially on Aid to Families with Dependent Children (AFDC), Medicaid, and state medical assistance programs, have consumed a major and increasing proportion of the city's Expense Budget.[3] Table 3 shows that in 1961 welfare expenditures' share of the budget was about 15 percent, whereas by 1975 it had increased to about 29 percent. For fiscal 1976, the total amount spent on social assistance was 3.69 billion out of a total Expense Budget of $12.55 billion, that is, about 29 percent of the total expenditure. Of this, $1.05 billion was spent for AFDC and

---

[3] This section leans very heavily on the Temporary Commission on City Finances, *Public Assistance Programs in New York City: Some Proposals for Reform,* Twelfth Interim Report to the Mayor, February 1977, pp. 75–77.

about $1.86 billion for Medicaid and state medical assistance programs.

One of the reasons for the spiraling expenditures on social welfare was that the city has very little control over public assistance costs. New York State determines need standards, eligibility criteria, grant levels, and other conditions of public assistance. New York City is then required to administer these programs and finance a substantial proportion of the nonfederal share of their cost. The state requires that the city pay 25 percent of the AFDC cost and 50 percent of the cost of the Supplemental Security Income and general assistance programs. This requirement is unique. Only six other states require any local sharing of the costs of these three programs, and their formulas for cost-sharing are less severe for local governments.

Contributing to the city's burden for public assistance financing is the current federal reimbursement formula for the AFDC program. Under this formula, thirteen states, including New York, receive a 50 percent reimbursement, while other states receive a higher federal contribution. For example, Arkansas, Kentucky, Maine, New Mexico, Utah, and West Virginia are reimbursed for over 70 percent of AFDC benefit costs. The federal formula defines a state's "ability to pay" on the basis of its per capita income in relation to the national average, obviously a narrowly defined standard because it overlooks geographic variations in living costs, public assistance receipts, payment levels, and economic conditions. In the case of New York City, it neglects the special ethnic-racial composition of the population. States with low per capita income and AFDC benefits are favored by the federal formula while a state like New York is discriminated against.

Apart from some administrative improvements (for instance, in checking on welfare recipients to reduce cheating), the city cannot do much to reduce the burden of welfare costs without changes in the federal and state regulations.

Labor Costs. The largest item in the city's Expense Budget is labor costs, which include wages and salaries, fringe benefits, pensions, and social security taxes. Table 4 shows that between 1961 and 1975 total labor costs increased at a compound annual rate of about 11 percent. Over the same period, the consumer price index for the New York region increased at a compound annual rate of about 4 percent, and city employment increased about 2 percent, compounded annually. Allowing for this inflation and employment growth, the total real labor cost grew at a compound annual rate of about 5 percent. Compared with the state and the nation, this is certainly a high rate. More

TABLE 4

GROWTH IN NEW YORK CITY'S LABOR COSTS, FISCAL YEARS 1961–1977
(millions of dollars)

Fiscal Year Ending June 30	Personal Service[a]	Fringe Benefits[b]	Pensions[c]	Social Security Taxes	Total
1961	1,069.8	15.3	230.04	30.09	1,345.23
1962	1,152.2	16.9	258.73	33.39	1,461.22
1963	1,318.7	19.3	279.67	41.79	1,659.46
1964	1,457.3	15.9	303.44	43.45	1,820.09
1965	1,556.5	28.6	316.89	46.89	1,948.88
1966	1,609.6	55.7	362.03	70.91	2,098.24
1967	1,906.3	78.1	392.56	74.77	2,471.73
1968	2,109.7	93.1	422.45	95.82	2,721.07
1969	2,278.9	113.9	433.29	111.70	2,937.79
1970	2,769.7	141.8	504.43	119.22	3,535.15
1971	3,082.8	160.7	609.82	131.41	3,984.73
1972	3,271.4	175.9	633.58	159.56	4,240.44
1973	3,591.5	241.0	638.43	200.77	4,671.70
1974	3,791.9	261.5	895.66	225.15	5,174.21
1975	4,122.7	282.9	887.16	253.15	5,545.91
1976	N.A.	N.A.	1,229.98	250.00	—
1977	N.A.	N.A.	1,430.76	255.00	—
Compound annual growth rate (percent)	10.12[d]	23.17[d]	12.10	14.29	10.65[d]

[a] Excludes wages and salaries paid to employees of the municipal hospital system.
[b] Includes only major fringe benefits, health insurance, welfare funds, and uniform allowances.
[c] Includes contributions to union annuity funds.
[d] Computed for the period 1961–1975.
SOURCE: Temporary Commission on City Finances, *Sixth Interim Report*, May 1976, and *Final Report to the Mayor of New York City*, May 1977.

importantly, some of the components of the total labor cost showed even higher rates of growth. In nominal terms, over the period 1961–1975, fringe benefits grew at the rate of 23.2 percent, pensions at 10.1 percent (12.1 percent if fiscal 1976 and 1977 are included), and total social security taxes at 16.4 percent, all compounded annually. Taking into account inflation and employment growth, these growth rates were about 17 percent (fringe benefits), 4 percent (pensions), and 10 percent (social security taxes). By any measure, these are impressive—and disturbing—figures.

What makes labor costs so important in the city's Expense Budget is that they are charged against the city's own tax revenues, which have grown at a much slower rate than have labor costs. For Medicaid, AFDC, and other social assistance programs, the city receives substantial aid from the federal and state governments. But there is no such aid for labor costs. Since these costs are the largest single item in the Expense Budget, the city cannot avoid recurring budget crises unless ways are found to reduce them.

Total labor cost can be reduced if its components—wages and salaries, fringe benefits, pensions, and social security taxes—can be controlled. Significant steps have already been taken in this direction by reducing pension outlays. In 1971 Governor Nelson Rockefeller established the Permanent Commission on Public Employee Pension and Retirement Systems, which then set up a program that applies to all public employees in the state appointed after June 30, 1973. Under this program, pension costs are reduced by integrating social security benefits with retirement benefits. In addition, pension benefits are related to a three-year final average salary rather than to the salary just before retirement, and longer service is required to receive full benefits. This study examines in depth the role of pensions and social security taxes in the New York City fiscal crisis.[4]

---

[4] The role of fringe benefits in the city's fiscal crisis was studied in the Temporary Commission on City Finances, *The Fiscal Impact of Fringe Benefits and Leave Benefits: Some Proposals for Reform*, Seventh Interim Report to the Mayor, June 1976.

2

Trends in City Retirement Costs

New York City has five major actuarial pension systems and a few minor ones. These are described in detail in Appendix A and their respective benefits in Appendix B. In this chapter we consider the costs of the benefits of the five pension systems as reported by the city, their growth over the past several years, the reasons for their growth, and how the costs are financed.

Total Retirement Costs

New York City's contributions to pension funds, to union annuity funds, and to social security taxes—the three components of retirement costs—are shown in summary form in Table 5. Each of these components has shown a significant upward trend. Their compound annual growth rates are 11.9 percent for pensions (13.3 percent for the five actuarial systems), 78.4 percent for union annuity funds (1966–1977), and 14.3 percent for social security taxes. Total retirement costs, including actuarial and nonactuarial systems, have increased at a compound annual rate of 12.4 percent.

The growth rates covering the period 1961–1977 are substantial, but in most cases the rate of growth has accelerated since about 1969. For example, between 1970 and 1977 the city's contribution to the New York City Employees' Retirement System (NYCERS) grew at a compound annual rate of about 21 percent; the corresponding rate for the Teachers' Retirement System (TRS) was 20 percent.

As noted in chapter 1, all components of retirement costs have increased faster than the city's revenues. But since these costs are supposed to be paid out of tax levy money only, one should compare retirement costs with the tax levy and not with total revenue, for the

11

TABLE 5

Retirement Benefit Costs of New York City Pension Systems, Fiscal Years 1961–1977

(millions of dollars)

Pension System	1961	1962	1963	1964	1965	1966	1967	1968	1969
Major actuarial systems									
NYCERS	68.01	70.40	67.73	80.18	68.50	96.08	109.71	110.00	128.39
TRS	64.09	72.33	90.37	92.47	96.67	101.04	98.70	112.76	103.48
Police	23.23	24.25	26.68	30.60	46.66	56.44	68.38	75.70	47.09
Fire	9.46	11.69	12.97	14.87	19.15	22.92	23.55	22.27	31.28
BERS	3.25	2.96	3.92	4.92	5.51	5.59	5.52	5.92	4.85
Total	168.04	181.63	201.67	223.04	236.49	282.07	305.86	326.65	315.09
Other actuarial	1.00	1.50	2.50	3.10	3.70	3.80	4.00	3.70	5.90
Nonactuarial	61.00	75.60	75.50	77.30	76.70	76.10	82.20	87.50	92.90
Total pensions	230.04	258.73	279.67	303.44	316.89	361.97	392.06	417.85	413.89
Social security taxes	30.09	33.39	41.79	43.45	46.89	70.91	74.77	95.82	111.70
Union annuity funds	—	—	—	—	—	0.06	0.50	4.60	19.40
Total retirement benefit costs	260.13	292.12	321.46	346.89	363.78	432.94	467.33	518.27	544.99

Pension System	1970	1971	1972	1973	1974	1975	1976	1977	Rate of Growth (percent)
Major actuarial systems									
NYCERS	157.72	222.44	294.79	254.51	316.66	296.79	455.89	604.70	14.63
TRS	101.99	140.69	32.70[b]	84.85	257.82	262.80	323.29	365.89	11.50
Police	85.01	80.28	95.95	88.26	97.54	97.90	174.99	200.36	14.42
Fire	31.86	32.04	33.32	40.57	38.10	43.10	51.20	50.90	11.09
BERS	6.05	8.52	9.38	10.20	11.07	12.06	16.28	13.93	9.52
Total	382.63	483.97	466.09	478.39	721.19	712.65	1,021.65	1,235.78	13.28
Other actuarial	7.40	9.88	16.27	15.94	18.17	17.32	34.76	27.13	22.91
Nonactuarial	93.60	87.37	121.42	110.60	120.90	121.99	138.57	132.85	4.99
Total pensions	483.63	581.22	603.78	604.93	860.26	851.96	1,194.98	1,395.76	11.93
Social security taxes	119.22	131.45	159.56	200.77	225.15	253.15	250.50	255.00	14.29
Union annuity funds	20.80	28.60	29.80	33.50	35.40	35.20	35.00	35.00	78.42
Total retirement benefit costs	623.65	741.27	793.14	839.20	1,120.81	1,140.31	1,479.98	1,685.76	12.39

[a] Annual compound rate of growth.
[b] The two-year lag was introduced for TRS in 1971. It existed for all other systems. This lag means that the actuarially determined contribution for any year is paid in the third year. Although this is done for "administrative" reasons, the real reason seems to be to defer payment until a later date for lack of money.

SOURCE: Temporary Commission on City Finances, *The Fiscal Impact of Retirement Benefits: Some Proposals for Reform,* Sixth Interim Report to the Mayor, May 1976, Appendix A, pp. 52–54.

latter contains a substantial amount of state and federal grants as well as some user fees and miscellaneous revenue.

Retirement costs consume an overwhelming proportion of the city's tax levy, ranging from 25 percent in 1961 to about 40 percent in 1975 (see Table 6). Over the same period the tax levy grew at a compound annual rate of about 7.7 percent, whereas pension costs increased at a rate of 9.8 percent, union annuities at 103 percent, and social security taxes at 11.1 percent, all compounded annually. This explains in part why the city has had to borrow repeatedly over the past several years.

Contributions to Major Actuarial Pension Systems

Although overall retirement costs have increased substantially, there are variations from system to system. Statistics are presented here for

TABLE 6

ACCRUED TAX LEVY AND RETIREMENT BENEFIT COST AS A PERCENTAGE OF TAX LEVY, FISCAL YEARS 1961–1975

Fiscal Year Ending June 30	Tax Levy Accrued (thousands of dollars)[a]	Retirement Benefit Cost as a Percentage of Tax Levy[b]
1961	1,028,352	25.30
1962	1,070,955	27.28
1963	1,134,556	28.34
1964	1,220,299	28.43
1965	1,313,910	27.69
1966	1,409,471	30.72
1967	1,573,316	29.70
1968	1,648,144	31.45
1969	1,737,903	31.36
1970	1,892,720	32.95
1971	2,080,474	35.63
1972	2,188,915	36.23
1973	2,468,196	34.00
1974	2,655,569	42.21
1975	2,896,176	39.37
Compound annual growth rate (percent)	7.68	—

[a] From the New York City *Comptroller's Annual Reports*, various issues; rounded to the nearest thousand dollars.
[b] Cost figures from Table 5.

14

the five actuarial pension plans in a standard form for the period 1961–1974 so that intersystem comparisons can be made easily. Data beyond 1974 on all the items considered below are not yet available owing to the three- or four-year lag in the publication of this information.

New York City Employees' Retirement System (NYCERS). The largest of the city's actuarial pension funds is NYCERS, described in Table 7. The employees' share of pension costs has increased only marginally, 2.4 percent since 1961, whereas the city's share increased substantially, 12.6 percent, both at compound annual growth rates. As a percentage of annual salaries, the employees' contribution to this pension has actually shown a dramatic decline, whereas the city's contribution has again shown a pronounced increase.

All the five actuarial pension systems are now on a two-year lag method of funding whereby the city's actuarially determined contribution for any given year is not made until two years later. Thus, the contribution for fiscal 1975 is made in fiscal 1977, and so on. Ostensibly, the reason for this lag is that it facilitates the administration of the systems in that it gives all concerned a period of time after the close of the year in which to ascertain the exact number of employees. The real reason is financial: it is a gimmick to avoid paying the contribution in the current fiscal year.

As a result of the two-year lag, the true magnitude of the city's burden of pension costs can be judged only by relating its contribution to pensions in any given year to the salaries prevailing two years earlier. This is done in column 9 of Table 7. Relating current contributions to current salaries (column 8) seriously underestimates the true burden of the city's pension cost. Column 9 shows clearly that over the last several years the city has been contributing about 17 to 18 percent of the employees' salaries to pensions[1]—an extremely generous contribution.

Column 11 shows that as a result of successive liberalizations of pension benefits, the average retirement benefits paid have increased considerably. In 1974 a retiree on the average got a pension of $4,137, about 36 percent of the average salary prevailing in that year, not taking into consideration the fact that retirement income is fully

---

[1] It is possible that there is a trade-off between pension contributions and pay increases, although this seems doubtful because annual salary increases have also been substantial.

TABLE 7

NEW YORK CITY EMPLOYEES' RETIREMENT SYSTEM (NYCERS), FISCAL YEARS 1961–1974

Fiscal Year Ending June 30 (1)	Number of Active Members (2)	Annual Rate of Salary (dollars) (3)	Average Annual Salary (dollars) (4)	Employee Contribution (dollars) (5)	Employer Contribution (dollars) (6)
1961	127,793	683,200,000	5,346	65,400,000	68,000,000
1962	131,656	735,404,623	5,580	60,966,554	70,397,097
1963	134,428	791,122,460	5,885	64,447,858	67,725,694
1964	136,214	850,783,009	6,245	65,559,360	80,177,405
1965	141,613	915,604,023	6,465	70,279,992	68,498,432
1966	147,439	1,020,809,347	6,923	76,510,779	96,081,086
1967	153,012	1,106,849,012	7,233	82,021,624	109,713,955
1968	158,395	1,227,422,474	7,749	85,646,028	109,996,586
1969	169,080	1,384,493,626	8,188	86,095,804	128,388,440
1970	182,520	1,587,189,146	8,695	87,691,686	157,723,634
1971	189,465	1,730,009,729	9,131	77,648,665	222,441,786
1972	190,037	1,850,135,857	9,735	78,847,759	294,787,283
1973	202,292	2,120,434,728	10,482	83,556,444	254,505,576
1974	208,455	2,372,493,669	11,381	89,175,901	316,664,023
Compound annual growth rate (percent)					
	3.84	10.05	5.98	2.41	12.56

SOURCE: Mayor's Management Advisory Board, *Pensions*, April 1976, Table 2, p. 50. Figures for 1961 are from the *Annual Report to the Superintendent of Insurance*, New York State, Department of Insurance.

exempt from the state and city income taxes and partly exempt from the federal income tax. Also, when social security benefits are added, this benefit as a percentage of preretirement earnings is much higher.

Teachers' Retirement System (TRS). Table 8 presents data on TRS comparable to those in Table 7. The pattern observed for NYCERS holds true for TRS, too, but the employer contribution as a percentage of current annual salary as well as the salary prevailing two years earlier is much higher.

Employee Contribution as a Percentage of Annual Rate of Salary (7)	Employer Contribution as a Percentage of Annual Rate of Salary (8)	Employer Contribution as a Percentage of Mean Salary in Second Prior Year (9)	Number of Beneficiaries on Rolls (10)	Average Amount of Annual Benefits to Retirees (dollars) (11)	Investment Income (dollars) (12)
9.57	9.95	9.91	19,444	1,723	47,200,000
8.29	9.57	11.03	21,104	1,798	54,021,240
8.15	8.56	10.19	22,772	1,871	59,873,623
7.71	9.42	11.30	24,040	1,938	65,887,915
7.68	7.48	8.97	25,157	2,016	72,310,623
7.50	9.41	11.70	26,312	2,106	78,442,038
7.41	9.91	12.42	36,667	2,165	86,174,215
6.98	8.96	11.36	30,534	2,361	94,981,813
6.22	9.27	12.07	31,766	2,576	105,760,659
5.52	9.94	13.51	35,722	2,923	115,513,038
4.49	12.86	17.03	40,478	3,310	131,646,867
4.26	15.93	19.84	46,723	3,732	144,850,077
3.94	12.00	15.34	49,020	3,924	165,172,556
3.76	13.35	17.69	51,638	4,137	186,875,095
—	—	—	—	6.97	11.16

The drop in the city's contribution from $140.7 million in 1971 to $32.7 million in 1972 and $84.8 million in 1973 was due to the introduction of the two-year lag method of funding into TRS in 1971 (all other systems had it before). In 1970 the teachers won major benefits from the city, the most important being a pension of 50 percent of the final salary after twenty years of service. In 1971 the city did not have money to pay the increased costs of the twenty-year retirement plan. Taking advantage of the two-year lag method of financing, the city postponed its payments until 1974, when it put a

TABLE 8

NEW YORK CITY TEACHERS' RETIREMENT SYSTEM (TRS), FISCAL YEARS
1961–1974

Fiscal Year Ending June 30 (1)	Number of Active Members (2)	Annual Rate of Salary (dollars) (3)	Average Annual Salary (dollars) (4)	Employee Contribution (dollars) (5)	Employer Contribution (dollars) (6)
1961	43,575	329,900,000	7,571	35,300,000	64,100,000
1962	43,638	366,613,746	8,402	33,019,929	72,330,734
1963	44,698	385,317,270	8,622	35,797,991	90,366,847
1964	48,621	429,708,870	8,838	37,334,821	92,472,779
1965	50,867	460,098,933	9,046	50,292,535	96,660,635
1966	53,867	517,535,072	9,608	41,301,843	101,037,713
1967	57,470	557,934,153	9,708	51,864,270	98,699,134
1968	59,204	614,205,818	10,375	35,053,192	112,759,006
1969	61,745	715,290,910	11,585	29,722,858	103,478,957
1970	67,027	859,294,096	12,821	35,827,769	101,994,680
1971	74,339	989,504,663	13,312	36,463,987	140,688,349
1972	76,116	1,105,236,243	14,523	38,225,298[a]	32,701,401[a]
1973	78,634	1,197,008,772	15,223	46,225,298	84,845,691
1974	81,349	1,324,868,670	16,296	52,241,640	257,819,050

Compound annual growth rate (percent)

	4.92	11.29	6.07	3.06	11.30

[a] The drop in the contribution is due to the introduction of the two-year lag method of funding.

SOURCE: Mayor's Management Advisory Board, *Pensions*, April 1976, Table 3, p. 51.

record $257.8 million into the pension fund, a jump of some $173 million over the previous year.

Column 8 of Table 8 shows that in 1974 the city contributed an astounding percentage of employees' salaries to the pension fund: 19.5 percent of the current salary and 24.6 percent of the salary prevailing two years earlier. Also, in 1974 the average retirement benefit of $6,919 was about 43 percent of the average salary prevailing in that year, not taking into account the tax-exempt status of this income.

Employee Contribution as a Percentage of Annual Rate of Salary (7)	Employer Contribution as a Percentage of Annual Rate of Salary (8)	Employer Contribution as a Percentage of Mean Salary in Second Prior Year (9)	Number of Beneficiaries on Rolls (10)	Average Amount of Annual Benefits to Retirees (dollars) (11)	Investment Income (dollars) (12)
10.70	19.43	27.39	16,461	2,958	35,200,000
9.00	19.73	24.69	17,296	3,197	40,120,796
9.29	23.45	28.60	17,645	3,348	44,654,579
8.69	21.52	26.55	17,870	3,530	49,787,060
10.93	21.01	25.71	18,215	3,675	55,513,238
7.98	19.52	24.79	18,657	3,851	61,287,986
9.30	17.69	22.18	19,122	4,022	68,058,538
5.71	18.36	23.07	19,647	4,205	75,598,756
4.16	14.47	19.24	20,068	4,293	80,436,938
4.17	11.87	17.40	19,864	4,400	84,272,335
3.68	14.22	21.16	21,274	5,115	90,709,288
3.46	2.96	4.15	21,607	5,744	93,906,249
3.88	7.09	9.18	23,571	6,496	92,503,144
3.94	19.46	24.62	25,065	6,919	102,175,585
—	—	—	3.29	6.75	8.54

Board of Education Retirement System (BERS). The statistical data for the BERS system, which covers nonteaching employees of the board of education, are given in Table 9. Over the years, the contribution of these employees as a percentage of salary has declined, while the employer contribution has increased substantially. However, compared with the other actuarial systems, employees of the board of education have contributed a larger percentage of their salary toward pensions. Also, their average annual salary growth of 5.8 percent is the lowest among the five city pension systems.

TABLE 9

NEW YORK CITY BOARD OF EDUCATION RETIREMENT SYSTEM (BERS), FISCAL YEARS 1961–1974

Fiscal Year Ending June 30 (1)	Number of Active Members (2)	Annual Rate of Salary (dollars) (3)	Average Annual Salary (dollars) (4)	Employee Contri- bution (dollars) (5)	Employer Contri- bution (dollars) (6)
1961	4,226	23,500,000	5,561	2,800,000	3,300,000
1962	4,316	25,230,325	5,846	2,525,672	2,956,965
1963	4,515	27,791,690	6,155	2,834,279	3,920,791
1964	4,872	32,331,445	6,636	3,274,179	4,923,525
1965	5,108	34,960,759	6,844	3,786,870	5,511,685
1966	5,207	38,198,692	7,336	3,992,882	5,594,157
1967	5,368	41,863,406	7,798	4,443,933	5,520,116
1968	5,664	44,399,005	7,838	4,514,535	5,119,745
1969	5,493	42,653,505	7,763	3,987,723	4,852,774
1970	5,688	51,323,215	9,023	4,577,513	6,054,585
1971	5,904	57,632,795	9,761	4,336,829	8,519,451
1972	5,946	58,996,629	9,922	4,510,439	9,331,807
1973	6,332	65,290,756	10,311	7,464,409	10,203,221
1974	6,370	73,835,569	11,591	5,319,683	11,072,527
Compound annual growth rate (percent)					
	3.21	9.20	5.81	5.06	9.76

SOURCE: Mayor's Management Advisory Board, *Pensions*, April 1976, Table 4, p. 52.

New York City Police Fund, Article 2. The data for the police pension fund (Table 10) show again a dramatic reduction in the employee contribution as a percentage of the annual salary, a steep increase in the employer contribution, and a significant increase in the benefits paid to retirees. In 1974 the retirement benefit was about 44 percent of the average salary then prevailing, not taking into account social security benefits and the preferential tax treatment of both benefits.

Over the period 1961–1974, the number of beneficiaries on the rolls increased at a compound annual rate of about 25 percent. This was no doubt due to the twenty-year, no-minimum-age retirement

Employee Contribution as a Percentage of Annual Rate of Salary (7)	Employer Contribution as a Percentage of Annual Rate of Salary (8)	Employer Contribution as a Percentage of Mean Salary in Second Prior Year (9)	Number of Beneficiaries on Rolls (10)	Average Amount of Annual Benefits to Retirees (dollars) (11)	Investment Income (dollars) (12)
11.91	14.04	16.68	880	2,273	1,700,000
10.01	11.72	13.85	927	2,323	1,917,058
10.20	14.11	17.28	963	2,385	2,117,043
10.13	15.23	20.21	1,017	2,450	2,375,545
10.83	15.77	20.79	1,053	2,517	2,703,760
10.45	14.64	18.61	1,131	2,565	3,042,736
10.62	13.19	16.41	1,193	2,639	3,423,339
10.17	13.33	16.18	1,247	2,725	3,899,931
9.35	11.38	12.12	1,351	2,903	4,438,959
8.92	11.80	14.04	1,448	3,117	4,802,584
7.52	14.78	19.57	1,589	3,379	4,774,457
7.64	15.82	19.86	1,728	3,600	4,985,890
11.43	15.63	18.73	1,865	3,760	5,592,853
7.20	15.00	18.99	2,028	3,892	7,233,769
—	—	—	6.63	4.22	11.78

plan as well as to the very generous provisions of the "heart bill." This act, which applies to police and fire department employees, presumes that any heart ailment is job related.[2] No attempt is made to find out whether a heart injury is really service connected.

Table 28 in Appendix B shows that between 1969 and 1974, 749 firemen retired from service because of accidental disability, whereas

---

[2] The heart bill was first introduced in the late 1960s, and since then it has been reenacted every year. Its rationale seems to be the "inherently" dangerous nature of the jobs performed by policemen and firemen.

TABLE 10

New York City Police Fund, Article 2, Fiscal Years 1961–1974

Fiscal Year Ending June 30 (1)	Number of Active Members (2)	Annual Rate of Salary (dollars) (3)	Average Annual Salary (dollars) (4)	Employee Contribution (dollars) (5)	Employer Contribution (dollars) (6)
1961	22,405	148,100,000	6,610	14,400,000	23,200,000
1962	23,132	173,817,014	7,514	17,473,266	24,246,577
1963	24,596	194,174,098	7,896	20,073,188	26,681,580
1964	25,265	206,809,052	8,187	17,853,399	30,603,745
1965	25,803	232,177,003	8,999	19,902,683	46,658,720
1966	27,219	244,968,225	9,000	22,713,614	56,442,637
1967	27,927	275,481,616	9,866	25,218,007	68,383,264
1968	29,359	293,772,609	10,009	24,113,903	75,702,007
1969	30,742	324,111,650	10,475	17,826,977	47,091,760
1970	32,129	369,142,182	11,492	19,765,819	85,007,467
1971	31,761	371,112,758	11,684	21,052,273	80,283,600
1972	30,631	389,233,248	12,707	22,102,060	95,951,175
1973	30,734	474,541,222	15,442	25,105,894	88,259,360
1974	32,299	522,176,461	16,171	26,436,138	97,540,871

Compound annual growth rate (percent)

	2.85	10.18	7.12	4.78	11.68

Source: Mayor's Management Advisory Board, *Pensions*, April 1976, Table 5, p. 53.

the city had expected only 31 to do so. The reason for this phenomenal increase is very simple. The normal retirement (after twenty years of service regardless of age prior to 1973, and now after twenty-five years of service) entitles a fireman or a policeman to only 50 percent of his final salary in pension, whereas if he retires under accidental disability, his benefits increase to 75 percent. From the city's viewpoint, the heart bill is obviously very costly. The city recently discovered that some employees who had retired as disabled were holding full-time jobs elsewhere and drawing substantial salaries. The city has undertaken an investigation of the matter.

Employee Contribution as a Percentage of Annual Rate of Salary (7)	Employer Contribution as a Percentage of Annual Rate of Salary (8)	Employer Contribution as a Percentage of Mean Salary in Second Prior Year (9)	Number of Beneficiaries on Rolls (10)	Average Amount of Annual Benefits to Retirees (dollars) (11)	Investment Income (dollars) (12)
9.72	15.66	18.02	486	3,704	7,000,000
10.05	13.95	18.84	667	3,592	8,411,446
10.34	13.74	18.93	418	4,543	10,402,688
8.63	14.80	19.01	1,442	3,918	12,342,973
8.57	20.10	25.36	1,756	4,103	14,633,727
9.27	23.04	28.15	2,079	4,319	17,673,453
9.15	24.82	31.16	3,225	4,516	21,439,049
8.21	25.77	31.73	3,941	4,662	26,076,164
5.50	14.53	18.10	5,030	5,008	30,582,414
5.35	23.03	29.87	5,330	5,147	34,911,342
5.67	21.63	25.99	5,816	5,376	41,721,423
5.68	24.65	27.68	6,874	5,988	44,016,000
5.29	18.60	23.85	7,817	6,425	47,682,400
5.06	18.68	25.66	8,999	7,122	53,515,325
—	—	—	25.17	5.16	16.93

New York City Fire Department Fund, Article 1–B. Although similar in many ways to the other pension funds, the Fire Department Pension Fund described in Table 11 is unique in that since about 1969 the employees have contributed a very small amount. The reasons for this will be explained in chapter 3.

Like policemen, firemen have been retiring in increasing numbers, thanks to the twenty-year, no-minimum-age retirement plan and the heart bill. It is fair to say that although all the five pension plans are generous to their members, the police and fire pension plans are the most generous in terms of both the benefit structure and the cost to the employees.

TABLE 11

NEW YORK CITY FIRE DEPARTMENT PENSION FUND, ARTICLE 1–B, FISCAL YEARS 1961–1974

Fiscal Year Ending June 30 (1)	Number of Active Members (2)	Annual Rate of Salary (dollars) (3)	Average Annual Salary (dollars) (4)	Employee Contribution (dollars) (5)	Employer Contribution (dollars) (6)
1961	9,781	64,100,000	6,554	3,900,000	9,500,000
1962	10,275	77,408,959	7,533	4,479,799	11,689,469
1963	11,240	89,064,689	7,923	5,414,756	12,974,756
1964	11,659	96,230,339	8,253	3,846,530	14,870,355
1965	11,709	106,297,407	9,085	3,996,486	19,149,386
1966	12,026	111,026,044	9,236	4,276,645	22,922,201
1967	12,190	124,349,507	10,200	4,764,623	23,549,984
1968	12,294	126,232,514	10,271	4,910,356	22,266,846
1969	12,937	139,740,598	10,807	920,577	31,276,369
1970	13,494	155,861,730	11,553	476,853	31,859,829
1971	13,603	158,869,718	11,681	607,609	32,038,927
1972	13,337	169,945,762	12,749	499,044	33,321,365
1973	13,433	208,172,436	15,500	602,239	40,574,057
1974	13,382	226,808,086	16,951	608,899	38,093,520
Compound annual growth rate (percent)	2.44	10.21	7.58	−13.31	11.27

SOURCE: Mayor's Management Advisory Board, *Pensions*, April 1976, Table 6, p. 54.

Financing of Pension Costs

In order to understand why the city's pension costs have soared, it is necessary to consider its way of financing pension benefits. There are three major sources of money: income from the pension fund assets, employee contributions, and the city contribution.

Income from Plan Assets. Column 12 of Tables 7 through 11 gives for each pension fund the income it derives from investment. This information for all funds is shown in summary form in Table 12.

24

Employee Contribution as a Percentage of Annual Rate of Salary (7)	Employer Contribution as a Percentage of Annual Rate of Salary (8)	Employer Contribution as a Percentage of Mean Salary in Second Prior Year (9)	Number of Beneficiaries on Rolls (10)	Average Amount of Annual Benefits to Retirees (dollars) (11)	Investment Income (dollars) (12)
6.08	14.82	20.24	428	3,271	2,700,000
5.79	15.10	22.69	641	3,404	3,474,905
6.08	14.57	21.54	1,173	3,707	4,335,202
4.00	15.45	21.02	1,070	3,696	5,125,011
3.76	18.01	23.01	1,189	3,928	6,074,308
3.85	20.65	24.74	1,276	4,106	7,260,280
3.83	18.94	23.26	1,426	4,349	8,721,837
3.89	17.64	20.49	1,725	4,730	10,428,990
0.66	22.38	26.58	1,923	4,914	12,094,069
0.31	20.44	25.43	2,184	5,348	15,168,086
0.38	20.17	24.09	2,416	5,737	18,170,616
0.29	19.61	22.54	2,638	6,054	18,861,972
0.29	19.49	25.78	2,866	6,355	20,011,581
0.27	16.80	23.17	3,337	7,356	22,181,176
—	—	—	17.11	6.43	17.59

Investment income constitutes an important source of money in relative as well as absolute terms. Between 1961 and 1974, investment income grew at a compound annual rate of about 11.2 percent. Allowing for inflation, which was about 4 percent, this growth rate was about 7.2 percent. Whether this is an impressive rate of growth and whether the pension funds were prudently invested are important questions that deserve a special study and are therefore beyond the scope of this monograph. However, a recent study by the city comptroller has raised serious questions about the investment performance of three of four investment advisers to the city pension funds.

TABLE 12

INVESTMENT INCOME AND CITY AND EMPLOYEE CONTRIBUTIONS TO THE FIVE ACTUARIAL SYSTEMS, FISCAL YEARS 1961–1976

(thousands of dollars)

Fiscal Year Ending June 30	Employee Contribution		City Contribution			Investment Income
	Amount	Percent of year-end salary	Amount	Percent of year-end salary	Percent of mean salary in second prior year	
1961	121,800	9.75	168,100	13.46	16.15	93,800
1962	118,465	8.59	181,621	13.18	16.03	107,945
1963	128,568	8.64	201,670	13.56	16.74	121,383
1964	127,868	7.91	223,479	13.80	16.98	135,518
1965	148,259	8.48	236,479	13.52	16.50	151,236
1966	148,796	7.70	282,078	14.60	18.80	167,706
1967	168,312	7.99	305,866	14.52	18.18	187,817
1968	154,238	6.69	326,644	14.16	17.74	210,986
1969	138,554	5.32	315,088	12.09	15.60	233,313
1970	148,340	4.91	382,640	12.66	17.34	254,667
1971	140,109	4.24	483,972	14.63	19.70	287,023
1972	144,185	4.03	466,093	13.04	16.56	306,620
1973	163,197	4.01	478,385	11.77	15.12	330,962
1974	173,782	3.84	721,190	15.95	20.96	371,981
1975	N.A.	N.A.	712,000	N.A.	N.A.	N.A.
1976	N.A.	N.A.	1,021,000	N.A.	N.A.	N.A.
Compound annual growth rate (percent)						
1961–1974	2.78	—	11.85	—		—
1961–1976	—		12.78			11.18

SOURCE: Mayor's Management Advisory Board, *Pensions*, April 1976, various tables.

TABLE 13

City's and Employees' Contribution to Pension Systems as a Percentage of Annual Salary, Fiscal Years 1961–1974

Fiscal Year Ending June 30	NYCERS		TRS		Police		Fire		BERS	
	Employee	City	Employee	City	Employee	City	Employee	City	Employee	City
1961	9.57	9.95	10.70	19.43	9.72	15.66	6.08	14.82	11.91	14.04
1962	8.29	9.57	9.00	19.73	10.05	13.95	5.79	15.10	10.01	11.72
1963	8.15	8.56	9.29	23.45	10.34	13.74	6.08	14.57	10.20	14.11
1964	7.71	9.42	8.69	21.52	8.63	14.80	4.00	15.45	10.13	15.23
1965	7.68	7.48	10.93	21.01	8.57	20.10	3.76	18.01	10.83	15.77
1966	7.50	9.41	7.98	19.52	9.27	23.04	3.85	20.65	10.45	14.64
1967	7.41	9.91	9.30	17.69	9.15	24.82	3.83	18.94	10.62	13.19
1968	6.98	8.96	5.71	18.36	8.21	25.77	3.89	17.64	10.17	13.33
1969	6.22	9.27	4.16	14.47	5.50	14.53	0.66	22.38	9.35	11.38
1970	5.52	9.94	4.17	11.87	5.35	23.03	0.31	20.44	8.92	11.80
1971	4.49	12.86	3.68	14.22	5.67	21.63	0.38	20.17	7.52	14.78
1972	4.26	15.93	3.46	2.96	5.68	24.65	0.29	19.61	7.64	15.82
1973	3.94	12.00	3.88	7.09	5.29	18.60	0.29	19.49	11.43	15.63
1974	3.76	13.35	3.94	19.46	5.06	18.68	0.27	16.80	7.20	15.00

Source: Tables 7 through 11.

Employee and City Contributions. Table 12 also shows the employee and city contributions to the five actuarial pension funds. Although in absolute terms both these contributions are sizable, in relative terms the city's contribution has increased much more—a compound annual rate of about 12 percent compared with about 2.8 percent for employee contributions.

Expressed as a percentage of annual salaries, the employee contribution has declined steadily, whereas the city's has shown a dramatic upward trend (see Table 13). The fire department pension fund in particular has become practically noncontributory.

When the pension plans were established, the intent was that the employees and the city would share the costs equally. Over the years, and especially since 1969, the fifty-fifty cost-sharing principle has been diluted, with the city absorbing an ever-increasing proportion. The rapid escalation in the city's contribution started in the 1960s when, following the lead of the state legislature, the city introduced the ITHP scheme—Increased Take-Home Pay (see Appendix

TABLE 14

EMPLOYEE CONTRIBUTION TO RETIREMENT BENEFIT AS OF
DECEMBER 31, 1975

Retirement System	Average Rate of Employee Contribution as a Percentage of Pay	ITHP as a Percentage of Pay	Effective Employee Contribution (percent)
NYCERS			
Career	5.4	4.0	1.4
Transit	0	0	0[a]
Sanitation	6.7	5.0	1.7
Uniformed officers	6.9	5.0	1.9
Composite	4.4	3.4	1.0 (2.7)[b]
TRS	6.6	5.0	1.6 (4.1)
Police	7.2	5.0	2.2 (4.7)
Fire	5.3	5.0	0.3 (2.8)
BERS	5.6	4.0	1.6 (3.6)

[a] Since 1970 the transit workers do not contribute to their retirement system; the cost is fully borne by the city.

[b] Figures in parentheses are rates applicable since January 1, 1976, when in the face of the fiscal crisis the city reduced its ITHP contribution.

SOURCE: Mayor's Management Advisory Board, *Pensions*, April 1976, pp. 45–46.

B)—whereby an increasing percentage of the employee contribution was paid by the city. This is evident in Table 14, which gives the actuarially determined average level of employee contribution as a percentage of the annual pay and the part that is absorbed by the city through the ITHP provision. For, example, until the end of 1975, the average contribution of firemen was supposed to be about 5.3 percent of the annual pay, but, because of the ITHP offset of 5.0 percent, they contributed only 0.3 percent. Similarly, until December 31, 1975, the teachers and members of NYCERS contributed only a token amount to their pensions.

There is no question that the ITHP scheme has been expensive to the city. Table 15 shows how much the city could save by halving or eliminating the provision completely. By halving ITHP, the city

TABLE 15

ESTIMATED CITY CONTRIBUTION TO PENSIONS UNDER FULL, HALF, AND NO ITHP PROVISION, FISCAL YEARS 1977–1982[a]

(millions of dollars)

Fiscal Year	Contribution under Full ITHP[b]	Contribution under Half ITHP[c]	Contribution under No ITHP
1977	1,220.4	1,220.4[d]	1,220.4[d]
1978	1,257.2	1,210.4[d] (46.8)[e]	1,210.4[d] (46.8)
1979	1,300.0	1,206.5 (93.5)	1,113.0 (187)
1980	1,342.9	1,249.4 (93.5)	1,155.9 (187)
1981	1,385.7	1,292.2 (93.5)	1,198.7 (187)
1982	1,428.6	1,335.1 (93.5)	1,241.6 (187)

[a] Costs are based on computations for fiscal year 1977.
[b] 5 percent for teachers and uniformed employees and 4 percent for other employees.
[c] 2.5 percent for teachers and uniformed employees and 2 percent for other employees.
[d] Because of the two-year lag method of funding, the contributions are the same.
[e] The figures in parentheses represent savings as compared with full ITHP.
SOURCE: Temporary Commission on City Finances, *The Fiscal Impact of Retirement Benefits: Some Proposals for Reform*, Sixth Interim Report to the Mayor, May 1976, Table 20, p. 46 (savings computed by the author).

29

could save about $93.5 million annually by fiscal 1979; if ITHP were dropped completely, it could save about $187 million per year. These figures could be much higher, depending on the rate of growth of salaries and changes in actuarial assumptions.

Beginning January 1, 1976, the city cut its ITHP contribution in half. The Permanent Commission on Public Employee Pension and Retirement Systems as well as the Mayor's Management Advisory Board had recommended that the ITHP plan be dropped completely. Since ITHP is enacted annually, there is no question of constitutional guarantee of pension involved if it is abolished.

Since the employee contribution as a percentage of salary has been declining over the past several years, the pension plans could be made totally noncontributory. As a matter of fact, most private pension plans do not require any employee contribution. In the *1975 Study of Corporate Pension Plans* made by the Bankers Trust Company of New York (the tenth such survey), it was found that, out of a total of 271 private plans surveyed, about 182 or about 67 percent were totally noncontributory, about 19 percent allowed voluntary contributions, and only 14 percent required some contribution. However, their benefits were not as generous as those given by the five city pension funds, and most of them take into account social security benefits in determining their benefit structure. If public employee pension plans in New York City were made noncontributory, some fundamental changes would have to be made in their benefit structures. Without a substantial reduction in pension benefits, making the plans completely noncontributory would simply lead to an explosion in the city's pension costs.

Reasons for Escalating Pension Costs

Although ITHP is an important factor, it does not explain fully the city's rapidly mounting pension costs. The explanation must be sought in the rate of growth in city employment, the rate of growth of wages and salaries, and the nature of retirement benefits.

Employment Growth. Other things remaining the same, growth in employment will increase the total pension burden. Because employment figures for each system are not readily available, the number of members of the various systems may be used as proxies for employment. Tables 7 to 11 show that the compound annual rates of growth in membership for the period 1961–1974 were: 3.8 percent (NYCERS),

4.8 percent (TRS),[3] 3.2 percent (BERS), 2.9 percent (police), and 2.4 percent (firemen).

Although these growth rates do not appear to be exceptionally high, they are probably high when considered in light of the socio-economic changes taking place in the city. Middle-class families have been leaving the city for the suburbs in increasing numbers. Soaring crime rates, the continually deteriorating quality of the public schools, and higher taxes have contributed to the exodus. Similarly, many private corporations are moving out owing to the increasing cost of doing business in the city and the fact that corporate executives find the combined burden of federal, state, and city income taxes intolerable. The net impact of these developments has been a steady erosion of the city's tax base. On the other hand, the number of people receiving public assistance has increased dramatically, partly because of generous public assistance payment levels. In 1961, 4.4 percent of the city's population received some type of public assistance; this percentage jumped to 11.1 percent in 1968 and to 16.5 percent in 1975. In 1975 just about one out of every five people in the city received some public assistance. Against this backdrop, the employment growth rates for city employees might very well be quite high. In the face of declining enrollment in the city public schools, for example, what justification can be offered for the employment growth noticed for the TRS?

Salary Growth. Pension costs also increase as wages and salaries increase. Column 4 of Tables 7 to 11 show that the compound annual rates of growth of salaries and wages per employee for the period 1961–1974 were: 6.0 percent (NYCERS), 6.0 percent (TRS), 5.8 percent (BERS), 7.1 percent (police), and 7.6 percent (firemen). Between 1961 and 1974, the consumer price index in the New York area increased at a compound annual rate of about 4 percent. Allowing for this inflation, the salaries of most public employees showed a real increase of about 2 percent per annum, with policemen and firemen recording net increases of 3.0 and 3.6 percent, respectively. Whether these increases reflect productivity improvements is hard to say because of the difficulty of measuring productivity in the public sector.

Rise in Pension Benefits. The pension benefits of city employees have been liberalized over the past several years, especially since 1969.

---

[3] Because a majority of new college teachers belong to the Teachers Insurance and Annuity Association (TIAA), the recorded increase underestimates the true increase.

The twenty-year, no-minimum-age plan of the police and fire departments, retirement allowances based on the final year's salary rather than the average of the last three or five years' salary, and inclusion of overtime pay in the computation of the final pay are but a few examples of the ways in which pension benefits have been increased.

To illustrate the way liberalization of pension benefits leads to additional pension costs, consider the economic consequences of shifting from the five-year-average salary base to the final-year salary base in computing pension benefits. Consider the case of a first grade fireman (highest rank) with the following salary profile:

Year	Salary
1968	$10,000
1969	10,500
1970	10,950
1971	12,550
1972	13,362
Five-year average	$11,472

Suppose the fireman decided to retire in 1972 at age forty-five, after having served twenty years. Under the current provisions, his basic retirement allowance would be $6,681 (50 percent of the final salary of $13,362), whereas under the five-year-average salary method, his allowance would have been 50 percent of $11,472, or $5,736. The shift from the five-year average to the final salary nets the fireman $945 per year in additional pension benefits for the rest of his life. Assuming a life expectancy of twenty years at age forty-five and a rate of return of 4 percent per year, the present value of the annuity of $945 per year for twenty years is about $12,843.

In 1970 the city teachers won the right to retire at half pay after twenty years' service, the benefits to commence at age fifty-five. Until then, the minimum service requirement had been twenty-five years. A reduction in the service requirement from twenty-five to twenty means additional pension liability for the city unless the actuarially determined rate of contribution of teachers is increased to offset this change. But the city gave the benefit without requiring any additional contribution from the teachers. This is one reason why the city's pension contributions have soared since about 1969 when most of the pension benefits were liberalized.

One could estimate the actual dollar amounts of additional retirement costs resulting from reducing the retirement age, if profiles of members of the various pension systems by age, sex, years of service, and rate of salary were readily available. Unfortunately, the only source of this information is the Office of the Actuary of the City, but it is so overburdened with routine activities that it does not have time to publish the information or to do its own in-depth analysis of the true cost of the city's pension liabilities.

When pension benefits are increased, politicians and others concerned appear to pay very little attention to the potential costs involved. Since pension benefits are paid after retirement or disability, they are not as visible as wages and salaries. Section 50 of the Legislative Law of the State of New York, which requires that all public employee pension bills contain a fiscal note indicating the dollar impact of the changes proposed, appears to have had very little effect.

3

The True Cost of Pensions

The pension costs reported in chapter 2 and shown in Table 5, although sizable, do not reflect "true" pension liability because the city must provide whatever is necessary to pay the benefits promised even though the members' and the city's combined contributions are not sufficient to cover this cost. A policeman, for example, who retires after twenty years of service, regardless of age, is legally entitled to a basic retirement allowance of 50 percent of his final year's salary, whether his pension fund has the money or not.

Unrealistic Actuarial Assumptions

The reason that the city's true pension liabilities are greater than the reported costs of pensions is that its contributions to the five funds are based on actuarial assumptions that are hopelessly out of date. The linchpin of any sound actuarial pension system is the notion of "full current funding." This means that the annual payments to a pension fund must approximately equal the cost of benefits accrued by the employees during that year. Full current funding means that a pension fund has on hand, at the time a member retires and starts drawing benefits, an amount such that when it is invested at an appropriate (prevailing) interest rate, it will provide all future benefits owed that employee. The full funding principle has a number of advantages:

This discussion draws heavily on *Financing the Public Pension Systems, Part I: Actuarial Assumptions and Funding Policies*, prepared for the Permanent Commission on Public Employee Pension and Retirement Systems, New York State, March, 1976 (hereafter, *Assumptions and Policies*).

- It assures that costs of government services are paid for by the taxpayers who receive such services, rather than imposed on future generations.
- It assures public employees that the money will be available to pay the pensions they have been promised.
- It disciplines the bargaining process through which pension promises are made by requiring a current cash outlay to back up current promises.[1]

When the city's five actuarial pension systems were established, the notion of full current funding was clearly stated in their statutes. Despite this, none of them is funded at the rate at which liabilities are being accrued. This has resulted in a regular increase in the city's contribution, as a percentage of payroll, even in years when there was no improvement in the benefits. All this can be seen vividly in column 9 of Tables 7 to 11.

Full current funding requires that the pension funds determine as accurately as possible the full costs of promised benefits so that sufficient money can be contributed on a regular basis. An actuary can make this determination quite accurately, provided that reasonable assumptions are employed. One chief actuary, an employee of the city, does the forecasting for all the five pension systems, taking into account assumptions concerning mortality, employee turnover, disability, salary levels, and interest rates.

The reason the city pension plans are in trouble is that they have not kept their actuarial assumptions up to date. Most of the assumptions used currently were first developed for a 1914–1918 Commission on City Pensions and were based on the city's records of experience about mortality and so on for the period 1908–1914. Records from this period are still used for the TRS and even for the police and fire departments' pension funds, although the latter two were not established until 1940. Some slight changes were made in the 1940s regarding mortality rates after retirement and interest rate credits, but no other changes have been instituted—despite the fact that the city's chief actuary has made periodic reviews of the actual experience relating to mortality, disability, employee turnover, and so on and has noted the need for updating the actuarial assumptions. In virtually every annual report in the past several years, the chief actuary has made statements in language similar to the following:

The experience since the last actuarial investigation indicates the need for changes in the active service tables, salary scales

---

[1] *Assumptions and Policies*, p. 5.

TABLE 16

ACTUAL MORTALITY AS A PERCENTAGE OF ASSUMED MORTALITY, NEW YORK CITY PENSION SYSTEMS, VARIOUS YEARS

Pension System	Year of Latest Experience Study	Service Pensioners		Disability Pensioners		Active Employees	
		Men	Women	Men	Women	Men	Women
NYCERS	1970	73.8	62.2	59.5	73.4	40.3	18.6
TRS	1972	46.4	56.5	77.4	60.0	54.2	24.5
Police	1973	51.6	—	29.8	—	41.1	—
Fire	1969	21.3	—	12.5	—	36.5	—
BERS[a]	1971	99.8		94.3		46.1	

[a] Men and women combined.

SOURCE: *Assumptions and Policies*, Tables 1–3, pp. 16–18.

and the pensioners' mortality tables and studies leading to the preparation of new tables will be made. When new tables reflecting current experience have been determined, a report will be presented to the Board for appropriate action.[2]

Such tables have never been prepared. The trustees of the various pension systems are probably not anxious to adopt new tables, since that would require increased contributions by both the city and the employees.

Mortality Assumptions. Table 16 reports actual mortality as a percentage of assumed mortality for three categories of people: service pensioners (that is, those retiring after completing the minimum required service), disability pensioners, and active employees. All the pension funds overestimate the death rates for all three categories. In some cases, such as in the fire department system, the error is huge: in 1969 the death rate among disability pensioners was only 13 percent of the assumed rate and that of service pensioners only 21 percent. The consequences of overestimating mortality rates are serious. The city has to pay for the benefits of those retirees who outlive the systems' mortality assumptions.

Turnover Assumptions. Other things remaining the same, the larger the turnover rate, the lower the cost of providing retirement benefits.

---

[2] Ibid., p. 12.

TABLE 17

ACTUAL WITHDRAWALS AS A PERCENTAGE OF ASSUMED WITHDRAWALS,
NEW YORK CITY PENSION SYSTEMS, VARIOUS YEARS

Pension System	Year of Latest Experience Study	Men	Women
NYCERS	1970	63.1	102.0
TRS	1972	144.8	118.4
Police	1973	115.4	—
Fire	1969	21.4	—
BERS[a]	1971	188.9	

[a] Men and women combined.

SOURCE: *Assumptions and Policies*, Table 4, p. 19.

Table 17 shows that, again, there are glaring discrepancies between the actual and the assumed turnover rate for the five pension systems. The actual rate among firemen was about one-fifth the assumed rate, an error of 500 percent. Such underestimation increases pension costs because the city will have to contribute additional money for those who do not leave employment as expected. If the city had updated its turnover assumptions more frequently, perhaps it could have avoided such gross errors.

Disability Assumptions. The city's assumptions regarding nonservice disability and service-connected or accidental disability are also out of touch with the actual experience, as Table 18 shows. For the NYCERS, TRS, and BERS employees, nonservice disability retirement was overesimated for men, whereas for firemen and policemen it was underestimated, the rate of underestimation for policemen being about 44 percent. Concerning service-connected accidental disability, the errors are truly shocking. The actual accidental retirement rate is nine times the assumed rate for firemen and six times the assumed rate for policemen. In cases of accidental disability, policemen and firemen receive 75 percent of the final year's salary in basic retirement allowance, of which $5,200 is exempt from the federal income tax, whereas the nonservice disability allowance is 50 percent of the last year's salary, and all of it is taxable. By seriously underestimating the accidental disability rate, the city has created a severe funding problem, the more so because it has to pay 25 percent more in retirement benefits for an accidental disability than for a nonservice disability.

The 1973 experience for policemen and the 1969 experience for

TABLE 18

ACTUAL DISABILITY AS A PERCENTAGE OF ASSUMED DISABILITY, NEW YORK CITY PENSION SYSTEMS, VARIOUS YEARS

Pension System	Year of Latest Experience Study	Nonservice Disability		Service-Connected or Accidental Disability	
		Men	Women	Men	Women
NYCERS	1970	49.6	104.2	—	—
TRS	1972	70.3	25.6	—	—
Police	1973	143.3	—	610.0	—
Fire	1969	102.6	—	905.3	—
BERS[a]	1971	34.6		—	—

[a] Men and women combined.

SOURCE: *Assumptions and Policies*, Tables 5 and 6, pp. 21–22.

firemen in regard to accidental disability is entirely out of line with the rest of the state. Excluding New York City, the state's actual accidental disability in 1971 was 98 percent of assumed accidental disability for policemen and 93 percent for firemen, although the heart bill provision applies all over the state. The boards of the two retirement systems in the city may be more generous in interpreting the heart bill.

Salary Assumptions. The actuarial assumption that has the greatest impact on pension costs concerns salary increases over the working life of the employees. Table 19 shows how unrealistic these assumptions are. For policemen and firemen the actual rate of salary increase was about six times the assumed rate. The fire department fund's financial health is so poor that the city actuary cannot certify it as being actuarially sound. The reason for this is that in 1951, Section B19–7.65 of the Administrative Code of the City of New York was amended to provide that the city would make an annual contribution to the fund at three times the rate of contribution of the firemen. The combined payments were supposed to be adequate to provide the retirement benefits promised, but the actuarial assumptions regarding salary growth, disability retirement, and so on proved to be so unrealistic that the contribution rates have been found to be too low. Contributions have not been increased, however, because of an impasse over who will pay the increase. The matter may eventually be

TABLE 19

ACTUAL AND ASSUMED AVERAGE SALARY INCREASES, NEW YORK CITY PENSION SYSTEMS, VARIOUS YEARS

Pension System	Actual Annual Average Percent Salary Increase	Assumed Annual Average Percent Salary Increase[a]
NYCERS	6.2[b]	1.0[c]
TRS	7.2[d]	2.4
Police	9.1[d]	1.5
Fire	9.1[d]	1.6
BERS	6.1[b]	1.3

[a] Average of rates for men in age groups 25–55, 30–55, and 35–55.
[b] Based on annual average increase for 1969–1973.
[c] Clerks.
[d] Based on annual average increase for 1970–1974.
SOURCE: *Assumptions and Policies*, Table 9, p. 27.

settled in court. This impasse has led to a dramatic decline in the firemen's contribution to their pension fund, as column 5 of Table 11 shows.

Interest Rate Assumptions. Interest rates figure crucially in the computation of the present value of future benefits as well as in the return the city pension funds received on their investments. The interest rate that the pension funds use for actuarial purposes is fixed by law at 4 percent, which is very low compared with the present rates. If the funds had adopted realistic interest rate assumptions, the city's contributions could have been reduced.

Although higher interest rates would offset the cost increases necessitated by the other actuarial assumptions, it is debatable whether the offset would be sizable. The Mayor's Management Advisory Board on city pensions has concluded that even if the city recognized higher interest rates, it would have to contribute substantially more than it does now if it were to update the other four actuarial assumptions. However, this is an area that needs further study.

Fiscal Impact of Actuarial Assumptions

Given these unrealistic actuarial assumptions, we might ask whether the city pension funds are financially sound. One measure of sound-

TABLE 20

ASSETS AND LIABILITIES OF NEW YORK CITY PENSION SYSTEMS, FISCAL YEARS 1967, 1970, AND 1973

(millions of dollars)

Pension System	Total Assets	Reserve for Employee Contributions	Reserve for Retired Members	Assets Remaining for Active Members	Liability for Active Members	Percentage of Active Liability Funded
NYCERS						
1967	2,298	757	499	1,042	2,094	49.8
1970	2,738	777	1,032	929	3,912	23.7
1973	3,329	732	1,991	606	4,583	13.2
TRS						
1967	1,788	495	740	553	1,380	40.1
1970	2,073	493	794	786	3,277	24.0
1973	2,326	469	1,484	373	4,178	8.9
Police						
1967	576	131	192	254	1,118	22.7
1970	796	130	348	318	1,540	20.6
1973	1,072	145	611	316	1,987	15.9
Fire[a]						
1967	239	45	77	117	582	20.2
1970	342	41	140	161	760	21.2
1973	453	39	209	204	1,048	19.5
BERS						
1967	92	32	26	34	77	43.7
1970	106	33	38	34	141	24.4
1973	117	32	62	23	152	15.0

[a] This fund covers only firemen hired on or after March 1940. Obviously, the ratio of retirees to actives will increase significantly as the plan matures.

SOURCE: *Assumptions and Policies*, Table 10, p. 38.

TABLE 21

New York City Pension Systems, Cost Estimates, Fiscal Year 1976
(amount in millions of dollars)

| Pension System | Mean Salary July 1974–June 1975 | Costs as Currently Determined[a] | | Revised Costs by Alternative Funding Methods | | | | | |
| | | | | Entry age plus 40 years' past service funding | | Entry age plus 30 years' past service funding | | Aggregate current funding method | |
		Amount	Percent of salary	Amount	Percent of salary	Amount	Percent of salary	Amount	Percent of salary
NYCERS	2,453.6	588.0	24.0	627.4	25.6	648.4	26.4	816.3	33.3
TRS	1,385.7	380.9	27.5	473.4	34.2	490.6	35.4	506.9	36.6
Police	519.3	180.6	34.8	222.4[b]	42.8	228.8	44.1	244.7	47.1
Fire	219.4	50.9[c]	23.2	84.5[d]	38.5	86.8	39.6	90.6	41.3
BERS	77.0	20.0	26.0	20.9	27.1	21.5	27.9	25.4	33.0
Total	4,655.0	1,220.4	26.2	1,428.6	30.7	1,476.1	31.7	1,683.9	36.2

[a] That is, costs as determined by city actuary on present assumptions and present funding method.

[b] It is estimated that approximately $10 million per year or 4.5 percent of the annual cost of $222.4 million is the extra cost owing to the accidental disability benefits payable under the heart bill.

[c] Although the appropriate city contribution under the aggregate cost method and current actuarial assumptions would be $106.3 million, the recommended appropriation for fiscal year 1976 was $50.9 million. This is because the City Administrative Code specifies that funding shall be based on a contribution rate for each member (city share ¾; member share ¼), and no increase in the contribution rates had been voted by the trustees of the pension fund.

[d] It is estimated that approximately $7 million per year or approximately 8 percent of the annual cost of $84.5 million is the extra cost owing to the accidental disability benefits payable under the heart bill.

NOTE: Cost estimates based on June 30, 1974, valuation; 3 percent factor for general wage increments included.

SOURCE: Mayor's Management Advisory Board, *Pensions*, April 1976, Table A–2, p. 9.

ness is the unfunded accrued liability, which can be indicated by the ratio of assets on hand to the present value of future liabilities. If assets are 100 percent or more of liability, the funds are actuarially sound; if they are less than 100 percent, the pension funds are underfunded.

Table 20 includes the ratio of assets to accrued liability of members who are currently employed and not yet up for retirement. For all the pension systems this ratio declined between 1967 and 1973, the decline being particularly severe for the TRS. If this decline continues, the TRS may soon not have money to pay the benefits of those who are already retired, let alone the benefits of those who will retire in the future.

It is important to note that an unfunded accrued liability does not necessarily mean that a pension system is underfunded so long as the pension system makes additional periodic contributions reflecting realistic actuarial assumptions. Such contributions can be, and usually are, amortized over a period of twenty to forty years. But if up-to-date actuarial assumptions are not adopted, there is no way these pension funds can escape underfunding, with all the attendant consequences.

Table 21 includes estimates of how much the city would have had to contribute to the five pension funds in fiscal 1976 had it adopted the recommendations of the Mayor's Management Advisory Board. The city's actual contribution to pensions for that year was about $1,220 million, whereas alternative realistic assumptions would have required it to contribute between $1,429 million and $1,684 million. The more realistic assumptions would thus have cost the city from $209 million to $464 million. In terms of percentages, the city's contribution in 1976 was about 26 percent of the payroll, whereas it would have been between 31 percent and 36 percent of the payroll if the more up-to-date assumptions had been adopted.

In relative as well as absolute terms, the above figures are truly astronomical. As the Mayor's Management Advisory Board points out, the pension costs in private industry vary from 5 to 12 percent of payroll, or, if savings and profit-sharing plans are included, from 7 to 15 percent. The very heavy pension burden of the city is largely the result of the extremely generous pension benefits it provides.

4

Integrating Pension Benefits with Social Security

Social security taxes paid by New York City have grown rapidly over the past several years. Table 4 in chapter 1 shows that between 1961 and 1977 the city's cost of belonging to the social security system grew at a compound annual rate of about 14 percent. This increase, the product of a steady increase in the social security tax rate applied to a continually increasing taxable wage base, is entirely outside of the city's control. However, public employers have the option of withdrawing from the system after giving two years' notice to the Social Security Administration.

In the wake of the fiscal crisis, Mayor Abraham Beame informed the Social Security Administration in March 1976 of the city's intention to pull out of the system at the end of March 1978. His immediate objective was to save the city several million dollars in payroll taxes ($250 million in 1976). The withdrawal would also give city employees an increase in take-home pay, since they would not have to pay their part of the payroll tax.

In January 1977, however, the mayor announced that the city was not going to opt out of the system, although he did not withdraw the notice filed with the Social Security Administration. It now seems that his initial announcement in March 1976 may have been politically motivated; it may have been a ploy to pressure the unions into accepting certain cuts in their benefits. Whatever the motive, the question of withdrawal from the system has now become academic, because in June 1977 the New York state legislature passed a law prohibiting any municipality in the state from dropping social security coverage. Perhaps the legislature was not sure whether any public pension plan could duplicate social security's retirement, survivors', disability, and hospital insurance benefits at a cost less than the employer's share of the social security tax, which in 1977 was 5.85 percent of the taxable wages up to $16,500. The 1977 amendments to the Social Security Act direct the secretary of Health, Education and Welfare to undertake a study of the feasibility and desirability of including in the social security system employees who are not now covered in federal, state, and local government and nonprofit institutions. If a positive recommendation is made by the secretary, and if Congress accepts it, the question of withdrawing from the social security system will become truly academic.

What then can the city do to reduce its overall retirement costs? The 1976 Coordinated Escalator Retirement Plan integrating the city's pension benefits with social security benefits is the least that can be done. This plan now applies to all public employees of the state, city, and other local governments in the state employed after June 30, 1973. In this chapter we consider the need for such integration.

Retirement Income Targets

Granted that it is practically (and now legally) impossible for New York City to opt out of the social security system, how should the city regard social security benefits in granting its own pension benefits? Put differently, what should be the overall objective of the city toward the retirement income of its employees?

Our examination of the city's five actuarial pension systems shows that the benefits they provide are independent of the retirement income provided by social security. As a result, pension benefits and social security combined can be a sizable proportion of the salary of the city employee, as we shall see shortly. Should there be any upper limit to this proportion? It is reasonable to assume that the combined income from pension and social security should not *exceed* preretirement income for several reasons:

- Social security benefits are exempt from the federal, state, and local income taxes.
- Pension benefits of New York City's public employees are exempt from the state and city income taxes.
- A portion of the pension income (that arising from the employee contribution) is exempt from federal income tax.
- Under the present federal income tax laws, the retiree and his wife, if sixty-five and older, are entitled to a double personal exemption.
- The retiree no longer contributes to the city pension fund.
- The retiree no longer pays the social security tax.

46

- The retiree no longer incurs work-related expenses (lunches, travel, and clothing).

What then should be the retirement income goal? Taking into account the factors just listed, one can compute the equivalence between the pre- and postretirement income, as is done in Table 22.

TABLE 22

CALCULATION OF RETIREMENT INCOME EQUIVALENT TO PRERETIREMENT
INCOME FOR MARRIED COUPLES RETIRING JANUARY 1976,
VARIOUS INCOME LEVELS

Item	Income Levels				
Preretirement income	4,000	6,000	8,000	10,000	15,000
Federal income tax[a]	28	330	679	1,059	2,002
Federal OASDHI tax[b]	234	351	468	585	824
Preretirement income after personal taxes	3,738	5,319	6,853	8,356	12,174
State income tax[c]	4	43	89	139	262
Preretirement disposable income after federal and state personal taxes	3,734	5,276	6,763	8,217	11,912
Savings resulting from retirement[d]	544	816	1,088	1,360	2,040
Retirement income needed to equal preretirement disposable income[e]					
Amount	3,190	4,460	5,675	6,857	9,872
Percent of total preretirement income	80	74	71	69	66

[a] Calculated in accord with prevailing tax code.

[b] Old-Age, Survivors, Disability, and Health Insurance; for 1975, 5.85 percent on earnings up to $14,100.

[c] In 1974 state and local income tax receipts were 13.1 percent of federal income tax receipts. This percentage probably rose in 1975 because federal taxes were decreased while state taxes increased. Therefore, the percentage of preretirement income needed to maintain living standards is probably slightly overstated.

[d] Savings from retirement are based on the *Revised Equivalence Scale for Estimating Equivalent Income or Budget Costs by Family Type* (BLS Bulletin no. 1570–2, 1968). Consumption requirements for a two-person husband-wife family after retirement are 86.4 percent of those for a like family prior to retirement (age 55–64). Savings are therefore estimated at 13.6 percent of preretirement income.

[e] It can be assumed that retirement income for these income classes will not be subject to taxes.

SOURCE: Alicia H. Munnell, "The Future of Social Security," *New England Economic Review*, July-August 1976, Table VI, p. 18.

To a married employee retiring at age sixty-five, a postretirement income of $9,872 is equal to a preretirement income of $15,000, which is about 66 percent of gross income. Similarly, a postretirement income of $6,857 is equal to a preretirement income of $10,000. In these examples, a postretirement income in excess of $9,872 or $6,857 would be equivalent to more than 100 percent of the preretirement income.

TABLE 23

ANNUAL SERVICE RETIREMENT BENEFIT (AFTER TAX) AND SOCIAL SECURITY BENEFIT AS A PERCENTAGE OF INCOME IN FINAL YEAR OF EMPLOYMENT FOR SELECTED EMPLOYEE GROUPS IN NEW YORK CITY AGE 65 AND MARRIED

Pension System	Retirement Benefit Including Social Security as a Percentage of Income			
	$10,000 pretax	$10,000 after tax	$15,000 pretax	$15,000 after tax
Twenty years of service				
NYCERS (career)	97	116	81	103
Transit twenty-year plan	117	140	97	123
Sanitation twenty-year plan	112	134	94	120
TRS	93	111	78	98
Twenty-five years of service				
NYCERS (career)	117	140	99	125
Transit twenty-year plan	123	147	103	130
Sanitation twenty-year plan	120	143	102	129
TRS	121	145	103	131

NOTE: Retirement benefit includes estimated pension from RITHP credits where applicable. New York public employee retirement benefits are subject only to federal income tax. Tax is based on 1975 tax rates with standard deduction, single or married exemption(s), with additional exemption at age 65. Federal tax is computed as if entire benefit were financed by employer. Social security benefits are estimates for employees who work during 1976 and begin collecting benefits in 1977. Disposable income from final year's salary is after federal, New York State, and New York City income tax and FICA payment based on 1975 taxable salary base of $14,100 and tax rate of 5.85 percent.

SOURCE: Permanent Commission on Public Employee Pension and Retirement Benefit, 1976 Coordinated Escalator Retirement Plan of New York State, Tables 21 and 22 (hereafter, Co-Esc Plan).

Are City Retirement Benefits Excessive?

Table 23 gives net retirement benefits as a percentage of gross as well as net, or disposable, income for retirees at age sixty-five with twenty and twenty-five years of service. A married employee, aged sixty-five, who retires after twenty years with a final year's gross income of $10,000 gets from 93 percent to 117 percent of that in combined pension and social security benefits. Taking into account taxes and other factors listed previously, the retirement income ranges between 111 percent and 140 of the preretirement net income. In all the cases listed in Table 23, the net retirement income is in excess of 100 percent of the net preretirement income. The excess is even greater for those who retire after twenty-five years of service.

The annual service retirement benefit (after tax) and social security benefit as a percentage of after-tax income is higher in New York than in several other major cities, as shown in Table 24. It is interesting to note that for twenty years' service, Chicago, which does not subscribe to social security, pays only 37 percent of the preretirement disposable income in total retirement income, whereas

TABLE 24

ANNUAL RETIREMENT BENEFIT AS A PERCENTAGE OF DISPOSABLE (AFTER-TAX) INCOME IN FINAL YEAR OF EMPLOYMENT FOR CITY EMPLOYEES

City	After Twenty Years' Service	After Twenty-five Years' Service
New York (career)	103	125
Chicago[a]	37	47
Dallas[a]	42	52
Denver	84	91
Detroit	94	104
Los Angeles[a]	44	54
Memphis[a]	44	54

NOTE: Annual benefit includes both retirement benefit (after tax) and social security benefit for general public employees, age sixty-five, married, with a final year's salary of $15,000. Disposable income estimates for cities other than New York City do not take account of any state or local income taxes due on salaries or retirement benefits. Social security benefits are estimates for employees who work during 1976 and begin collecting benefits in 1977.

[a] Employees not covered by social security.

SOURCE: *Co-Esc Plan*, Tables 25 and 26.

the corresponding percentage for New York City, including social security, is 103.

In sum, there is no doubt that in absolute as well as relative terms, the city's retirement benefits are excessive. This is so partly because the city does not have a coordinated pension policy. The three elements of retirement income—pension, special union annuity funds, and social security—are disparate entities, none related in any way to the overall benefits.

Integration with Social Security

One way the city could reduce its retirement benefit costs is to integrate its benefits with those of social security. As a matter of fact, as far back as 1963, the Martin E. Segal Company which the city hired to do an extensive study of its pension system concluded:

> The need for a new pension system becomes overwhelmingly obvious when future developments in Social Security are considered. . . . It is clear that one cannot fix an adequate retirement structure now without consideration of Social Security and expect it to make sense 10 years from now, much less 40 or 60 years from now.[1]

The city did not follow the recommendation of the Segal report until 1973, when it was forced to do so by the state. A new pension plan that incorporates social security benefits into the computation of benefits was instituted for all public employees in New York appointed effective July 1, 1973, and thereafter. We shall discuss the 1973 plan shortly, but in the meanwhile let us look at how the private sector deals with social security benefits.

Private Pension Plans and Social Security. Pension plans in the private sector generally use one of three types of integration formulas: offset formula, which takes into account a certain percentage of social security benefits; step-up formula, which has one benefit structure for salary subject to social security tax and another for the remainder; and excess formula, which is a variation of the step-up method in that pension benefits are provided only on compensation over the break-even point, usually the social security wage base. In the Bankers Trust Company's *1975 Study of Corporate Pension Plans*, it was found that out of 203 conventional pension plans studied, about 60 (30 percent)

---

[1] Martin E. Segal Company, Inc., *The Retirement Systems of the City of New York, Part Five: The Benefit Structure* (New York, 1963), p. 9.

used the offset formula, about 113 (56 percent) had adopted the step-up formula, about 4 (2 percent) used the excess formula, and only 26 (about 12 percent) were not integrated with social security. Thus, about 88 percent of the plans included in the study were integrated with social security in one way or another.

Table 25 gives the median plan benefits and social security benefits of the conventional plans for selected levels of income. At the lower income levels social security benefits are greater than private pension benefits; at higher income levels the reverse is true. But in none of the cases listed did the total retirement benefit exceed 68 percent of the final salary. Compared with these figures, the total benefits under the city pension plans given in Table 23 are extremely generous. (Note that the city benefits given in Table 23 are for twenty and twenty-five years of service. For thirty or more years of service, the benefits are still higher.) One reason these benefits are so generous is that, unlike private pension plans, the city completely neglects taking social security benefits into account, even though it contributes as much as an individual employee in social security taxes.

1976 Coordinated Escalator Retirement Plan

Alarmed at the growing public employee retirement costs at the local and state levels, Governor Nelson Rockefeller established in 1971 the Permanent Commission on Public Employee Pension and Retirement Systems. One of its major tasks was to devise a rational pension policy for public employees in New York State. Pursuant to its man-

TABLE 25

MEDIAN PENSION BENEFITS AS A PERCENTAGE OF FINAL YEAR'S
COMPENSATION[a] FOR THIRTY YEARS' SERVICE UNDER CONVENTIONAL
PENSION PLANS, 1975

Final Year's Compensation	Private Pension Benefits	Social Security Benefits	Total Benefits
9,000	29	39	68
15,000	32	25	57
25,000	35	15	50
50,000	38	8	46

[a] 5 percent annual salary increase used in computations.
SOURCE: Bankers Trust Company, *1975 Study of Corporate Pension Plans*, New York, p. 29.

date, the commission presented a pension plan which became effective for all public employees in the state appointed after June 30, 1973, and for previous employees who opted for it. This plan was refined over the next three years and a new plan, known as the 1976 Coordinated Escalator Retirement Plan, was then enacted. The new plan is, with a few exceptions, retroactive to 1973.

Among the salient features of the 1976 plan is that for the first time social security benefits are taken into account in providing retirement benefits. Since the public employer pays half the cost of social security, the new plan takes into account half the primary social security amount; benefits provided for the spouse are not considered, although the employer contributes indirectly to the spouse's benefit.

Most New York City and State pension plans did not have cost of living adjustment (COLA) provision for the retirement benefits, although social security benefits have been indexed since 1975. A second major feature of the 1976 plan is that it provides, for the first time, for indexing pension, disability, and survivors' benefits up to 3 percent per year. But maximum indexation applies only if all conditions of retirement or disability are fulfilled.

Another change is that pension benefits under the 1976 plan are related to the three-year final average salary and not to the salary prevailing in the last year or the salary just before retirement, as was the practice before.

In addition, the retirement age for general employees has been increased from fifty-five to sixty-two, although they are encouraged to stay on until sixty-five to claim full indexation of their benefits. Retirement between sixty-two and sixty-five qualifies for less than maximum indexation, and the COLA provision does not apply at all to those who retire before age sixty-two.

For the first time under the 1976 plan, a ceiling has been imposed on the retirement benefits of general employees. The maximum benefit is 60 percent of the first $12,000 of three-year final average salary plus 50 percent of the excess. These benefits are reduced if the employee retires before age sixty-two.

The policemen and firemen, in recognition of their hazardous jobs, can retire at any age after twenty-five years of service with full COLA benefits, but COLA is reduced to zero if retirement takes place after only twenty-two years of service. Under the previous arrangement, these uniformed employees could retire at any age after twenty years' service.

Finally, the new plan provides for an offset of one-half of

primary social security benefits attributable to the public employment of the disabled employee. COLA benefits are attached to disability benefits. One-half of primary social security plus Workman's
Compensation are taken into account in determining accidental disability benefits, which are also indexed.

In addition to this list of changes, the commission has recommended that the state prohibit the city from contributing to the
special union annuity funds and also that it abolish the increased-
take-home-pay (ITHP) provision so that city employees would pay
their full actuarially determined contribution toward their pensions.
As Table 27 in Appendix B shows, the city's contribution in 1976 to
the union annuity funds was about $36 million. From Table 15 in
chapter 2 it is clear that if ITHP were abolished beginning in 1979,
the city could save as much as $187 million annually. These two re-
forms alone could save the city in excess of $200 million annually. The
commission estimates that if all the recommendations made by it are
adopted, the city could save about $2 billion over the next ten years.

The Mechanics of Integration. To show how the new plan integrates
social security with system pension benefits for service retirement,
Table 26 presents an illustrative computation for a city policeman
or fireman. If he retires at age forty-six after twenty-five years of
service, his retirement allowance would be $8,928 under the old plan
but $7,650 under the 1976 plan. He thus loses about $1,278 immedi-
ately, although of course the city saves this amount. But over the
years, employees under the old plan will continue to receive the same
system benefit of $8,928, whereas those under the new plan will re-
ceive higher benefits as a result of the COLA provision. Thus, at age
sixty-two there is a difference of $1,193 in annual benefits in favor of
the employees who join the new pension plan.

In short, compared with the old plan, the retirement benefits
under the new plan are lower initially, but over the years they will be
much higher owing to indexing. Under either plan, however, employees get their indexed social security benefits.

It is questionable whether any pre–July 1, 1973, employees will
choose to join the new plan: the lengthened normal service requirement, the three-year final average salary as the basis for computing
benefits and the offset of half the primary social security retirement
allowance would work to the disadvantage of those who have already
put in substantial service. Employees who joined the public service
after June 30, 1973, have no choice; they must join the new plan
(college teachers, however, can join the TIAA plan, which is privately

TABLE 26

Retirement Benefits under the Pre-1973 and the 1976 Pension Plans
for a Police/Fire Employee Retiring at Age 46 with Twenty-Five
Years' Service at a Final Average Salary (fas) of $15,300

Estimated Benefit	1976 Plan		Pre-1973 Law	
	Amount (dollars)	Percent of fas	Amount (dollars)	Percent of fas
At age 46	7,650	50	8,928	58[a]
At age 56	10,281	67[b]	8,928	58
At age 61	11,918	78	8,928	58
At age 62				
City pension	10,121[c]	66	8,928	58
Social security	4,310	28	4,310	28
Total	14,431	94	13,238	86
At age 72				
City pension	13,602	89	8,928	58
Social security	5,792	38	5,792	38
Total	19,394	127	14,720	96

[a] Benefits 50 percent of fas for first twenty years and 1.67 percent for each year thereafter.

[b] Assumptions: 3 percent per annum esclation on Co-Esc and social security benefit, but no escalation on pension benefits for pre–July 1, 1973, employees.

[c] The figure is arrived at as follows: Discount social security of $4,310 back to sixteen years at 3 percent, which gives $2,686. One-half of this amount is $1,343. Subtract this from the fas of $7,650 to give $6,307. Compound this amount at 3 percent for the next sixteen years to obtain $10,121, which is the New York City system benefit.

Source: *Co-Esc Plan*, p. 29.

managed). It is with them that the future savings in the retirement costs will come about. It is too early to assess the impact of the new plan because of the hiring freeze imposed since the advent of the fiscal crisis; there is presently very little addition to the city payroll and many city jobs that were temporarily unfilled remain so because of the freeze. Nonetheless, the commission expects that over the next ten years the savings in retirement costs will be about $2 billion if all its recommendations, including the abolition of the ithp and union annuity payments, are implemented.

APPENDIX A

New York City's Retirement Systems

The city's fifteen retirement systems fall into two broad categories: actuarial and nonactuarial (or pay as you go).

Actuarial Retirement Systems

There are five major and three minor actuarial pension systems. Under these systems, annual contributions are made by the employer or employee or both on the basis of legally prescribed actuarial assumptions. These contributions, when accumulated into a reserve fund, are deemed sufficient to pay all the benefits that are due a member when he or she retires, either in a lump sum or as an annuity. The five major actuarial systems described here are the most important, both financially and politically.[1] (The details regarding benefits, costs, and so on of each system are discussed in chapter 2 and Appendix B.)

New York City Employees' Retirement System (NYCERS). The NYCERS, the largest of the five actuarial systems, was established on October 1, 1920, under chapter 427 of the Laws of 1920 of New York State. It is actually an amalgam of four subsystems, each of which has its own retirement plan and benefit structure. These subsystems cover career employees; transit operating employees; uniformed sanitation employees; and transit police, housing police, and the uniformed correction force.

Membership in the system is mandatory for all employees after six months of service. Originally under the supervision of the Board

---

[1] The following discussion is based on Thelma E. Smith, ed., *Guide to the Municipal Government of the City of New York*, 10th ed. (New York: Meilen Press, 1973).

of Estimate, the NYCERS was placed under a separate board of trustees in 1969. The membership of the board consists of the chairman (a mayoral appointee), the city comptroller, the president of the city council, presidents of the five boroughs of the city, and three public employee representatives. All members of the board are non-salaried.

The day-to-day operations are handled by the Bureau of Retirement and Pensions, which is run by the secretary of the retirement system, an appointee of the board. The financial aspects of the system are handled by a municipal banking and life insurance corporation, which operates under the supervision of the New York State Department of Insurance and is one of New York City's sizable financial institutions.

Teachers' Retirement System (TRS). The TRS was established on August 1, 1917. It is managed by a board consisting of the city comptroller, the president of the board of education, two appointees of the mayor (one of whom is a member of the board of education), and three teachers who are elected for a term of three years by the members who contribute to the system.

Membership in the system is mandatory for teachers employed by the board of education or the board of higher education and for certain administrative personnel. However, beginning in 1967 college teachers were allowed to join an alternative system—Teachers Insurance and Annuity Association (TIAA)—which is managed privately.

Board of Education Retirement System (BERS). The BERS, established on August 31, 1921, is open to those nonpedagogical employees of the board of education who are ineligible to join the TRS. The board itself governs the system.

Police Pension Fund, Article 2. Established in 1857, the Police Department Pension Fund is the oldest public pension system in the country. Originally, it was financed by funds obtained by the sale of unclaimed goods. Beginning in 1892, the policemen were required to contribute 2 percent of their salary to the fund, and the city provided the balance necessary to pay the benefits promised.

In April 1940 the management of the fund was entrusted to a board of trustees consisting of twelve members. These include the police commissioner, the city comptroller, a mayoral representative, the finance administrator of the city, and eight representatives of police organizations. Of the twelve votes cast, six are allotted to the representatives of the police organizations and six to the other members of the board.

Fire Department Pension Fund, Article 1–B. Although it dates back to 1871, this fund in its present form was established in August 1941. Its organizational structure is similar to that of the Police Department Pension Fund.

In addition to the five major actuarial systems, there are three minor ones.

Cultural Institutional Retirement System. The city contributes to this privately managed system on behalf of employees of the many cultural institutions, such as the Brooklyn Museum and the Metropolitan Museum of Art, that are partly funded by the city.

Library Employees Retirement Arrangement. Employees of the New York Public Library, the Brooklyn Public Library, and the Queens Borough Public Library are eligible for membership in the New York State Employees' Retirement System (NYSERS). The city contributes to NYSERS on behalf of the library employees.

Teachers Insurance and Annuity Association (TIAA). The TIAA is a privately operated, nonprofit retirement system for college teachers throughout the United States. Since 1967 the City University of New York faculty members have had the option of joining either TRS or TIAA, and about 75 percent of all new faculty members have chosen the latter. An important advantage of TIAA is early vesting and portability of pension benefits. The city contributes 12 percent of the salary subject to social security taxes and 15 percent of the balance.

Nonactuarial Retirement Systems

The nonactuarial retirement systems are funded on a pay-as-you-go basis. Benefits are paid to retirees out of the Expense Budget as they become due. The three principal nonactuarial systems are as follows:[2]

- Police Pension Fund, Article 1, covers members of the police department appointed before March 29, 1940.
- Fire Department Pension Fund, Article 1, covers members who joined the fire department before March 29, 1940.

---

[2] The following discussion leans heavily on New York City Temporary Commission on City Finances, *The Fiscal Impact of Retirement Benefits: Some Proposals for Reform*, Sixth Interim Report to the Mayor, May 1976.

- Relief and Pension Fund of the Department of Street Cleaning still covers those of its members who, as of December 1, 1929, did not elect to transfer to the NYCERS.

There are four nonactuarial funds whose membership is now frozen:

- The Health Department Pension Fund covers members of the fund as of October 1, 1920.
- The Supreme Court, First Department, Pension Fund is confined to those members who on October 1, 1920, did not elect to join the NYCERS.
- The Supreme Court, Second Judicial District Retirement Plan is confined to those members who on October 1, 1920, did not elect to join the NYCERS.
- The Grady Law Retirement Plan provides benefits for officers and employees of the city who are not entitled to the benefits of another city retirement plan.

Although it is not the purpose of this monograph to look into the workings of each pension system, there are a few general observations that may be made.

First, the fifteen pension systems are essentially disparate entities. Each sets its own rules and regulations regarding eligibility, retirement age, vesting provisions, disability and death benefits, and so on.

Second, although the city contributes very heavily to all the pension systems, it has very little effective control over them. The boards of the various systems retain all the power. Although this situation may have some advantages, the differing policies of the various boards regarding benefits, investments, and so on make it very difficult for the city to develop any coordinated pension policy. A strong case can be made for the establishment of a city pension office to oversee all the systems. At present, the only person concerned with the pensions is the chief actuary of the city, but his function is very limited: it is confined to the necessary actuarial calculations to determine a member's contribution rate to his or her plan. The chief actuary has no control over the investment policies of the various pension boards— in fact, he is not even a member of the various boards.

A final observation is that the investment policies of the various pension funds are also uncoordinated. For example, the NYCERS cannot own more than 3 percent of the total outstanding equity securities of any corporation. The corresponding limit for the Police Fund (Article

2) and Fire Fund (Article 1–B) is 2 percent. Similarly, the NYCERS cannot invest more than 1 percent of its assets in the securities of any one corporation or its subsidiaries. The corresponding limit for the police and fire department funds is 5 percent. It is strange that these practices exist, for although in theory the individual boards of the pension systems are responsible for the investment of their funds, in practice they have delegated this function to the city comptroller. There is no reason why the comptroller should not invest 5 percent of the assets of the NYCERS in the securities of a single corporation if he can do so for the police and fire funds. There is no question that such a disparity can work to the detriment of the individual pension systems in terms of the investment income they receive.

APPENDIX B

Benefit Structures of New York City's Retirement Systems

To understand the reasons behind the increase in the retirement costs of public employees in New York City, one must look at the benefit structures of the various pension systems. In this appendix we look at the nature of the benefits of the five major actuarial pension systems.

The retirement benefits fall into five broad categories:

- Service retirement allowance
    - (a) normal service retirement benefits
    - (b) early retirement benefits (vesting rights)
- Disability benefits
    - (a) ordinary disability benefits
    - (b) service-connected or accidental disability benefits
    - (c) social security disability benefits
- Death benefits
    - (a) ordinary death benefits
    - (b) accidental death benefits
    - (c) social security survivors' benefits
- Special benefits
    - (a) union annuity funds
    - (b) heart bill benefits
- Social security benefits (old-age pension)

Although the first four of these categories vary from system to system, social security benefits have been available to the members of all the systems since 1956, when the city joined the social security system.

The details of the retirement benefits of the five actuarial systems may be found in the New York State Commission on Public Employee Pension and Retirement System's publication, *Recommenda-*

tion for a New Pension Plan for Public Employees: The 1976 Coordinated Escalator Retirement Plan. What follows is a brief summary of the major features of the benefits prevailing before July 1, 1973. The changes made by the 1976 plan are discussed in chapter 4; they apply to the rather small number of employees who entered the city's service after July 1, 1973.

Service Retirement Allowance

As noted, there are two types of service-related allowances, one for normal service and another for early retirement, that is, retirement before the completion of the minimum normal service, which varies from plan to plan.

Normal Service Retirement Allowance. Basically, there are four categories of normal service retirement allowance. The first is the plan for 50 percent benefit after twenty years of service with no minimum age requirement. This plan is applicable to police, fire, and sanitation employees, transit and housing police, and the uniformed correction force. Employees in these categories who have put in twenty years' service, regardless of age, are guaranteed 50 percent of their last year's salary in pension benefits. This may be called the basic benefit. For periods of service above twenty years, additional pension benefits are accrued at a specified rate per extra year of service. For example, for the policemen, firemen, and transit and housing police, this rate is 1.67 percent of the final year's pay per year of service. Thus, a policeman who has worked for twenty-five years is assured of a minimum annual pension of 58.35 percent of his salary in the year of his retirement. In addition to the basic benefit and the benefit for years of service in excess of the minimum required, the retiree gets annuities from his contribution to the pension plan in excess of twenty years and from the city under the ITHP plan.

Before proceeding further, it is essential to point out the nature of financing the pension plans. Originally, when the pension systems were established, the idea was that both the employer and the employee would share equally in the cost of providing pension benefits. The contribution of the employee was based on the age at entry into service, sex, years of normal service, rate of growth of wages, and so on. But over the years this principle was diluted, with the city absorbing an increasing proportion of the employee's contribution. In 1960, following the lead of New York State, the city introduced the ITHP.[1] Under this plan, the city assumes a fixed proportion of the employee's contribution. For several years, these proportions were fixed at 5 percent of pay for uniformed personnel and 4 percent of pay for all other employees.[2] The amount thus calculated is put in a special reserve fund, called the reserve for increased-take-home-pay (RITHP). It should be pointed out that ITHP benefits are not permanent; they are sanctioned by the New York state legislature on an annual basis. As a matter of fact, in the wake of the fiscal crisis, the city halved its rates of contribution to the RITHP effective January 1, 1976.

An example is perhaps in order. Suppose that the actuarially determined rate of contribution for a policeman is 7.2 percent. But because of ITHP, the policeman contributes only 2.2 percent of his salary to his pension fund, the city contributing the remaining 5 percent on his behalf. (Effective January 1, 1976, the city contributes 2.5 percent, and the policeman contributes 4.7 percent.) The net effect of ITHP is thus to reduce the effective rate of contribution of the employee to the pension fund. Notice that under this scheme the policeman will contribute 2.2 percent (4.7 percent since the beginning of 1976) of his salary for twenty years (the minimum required under the policemen's pension fund), after which his contribution ceases, unless he decides to contribute voluntarily and get an annuity from this voluntary contribution. The city, however, contributes 5 percent (2.5 percent since January 1, 1976) as long as the employee remains on the job. Thus, if the policeman stays on the job for thirty years, he contributes to the pension fund for the first twenty years, whereas the city contributes for the whole thirty years. The employee is entitled to an annuity from the RITHP contribution in excess of the minimum service of twenty years, that is, for the last ten years in this example.

In short, the employee gets these retirement allowances: the basic allowance for the minimum service period, an allowance for years of service in excess of the minimum, an annuity from the RITHP

---

[1] ITHP was introduced in 1960 by the New York state legislature as an alternative way of granting wage increases in the wake of the 1960 economic recession. Since it is granted on a year-to-year basis, this type of wage increase does not lock the government into a permanent wage increase. However, ITHP has become in effect a permanent benefit, for since 1960 it has been passed by the legislature every year.

[2] Before January 1, 1976, the ITHP rates were as follows: NYCERS (career workers 4 percent of pay, transit workers 0 percent, sanitation workers 5 percent, and uniformed officers 5 percent), teachers 5 percent, board of education employees 4 percent, police 5 percent, and firemen 5 percent.

for service in excess of the minimum, and an optional annuity in case he had contributed voluntarily to the pension system beyond the period of minimum service. The same policy applies, with minor changes, to the other three plans discussed below.

The second normal service retirement plan allows a 50 percent benefit after twenty years of service with a minimum retirement age. This plan covers transit workers and teachers. The minimum retirement age is 50 for transit workers and 55 for teachers. Service after twenty years entitles the worker to 1.5 percent (transit workers) or 1.7 percent (teachers) of the final year's pay per year of service. Because the transit workers' pension plan has been totally noncontributory since 1970, they are not entitled to any ITHP annuity, but the teachers can get such an annuity for years of service beyond twenty.

The third of these plans allows a 55 percent benefit after twenty-five years of service. This plan covers nonuniformed employees and nonpedagogical employees of the board of education, that is, those not covered by the first two plans above. The benefit is 2.2 percent of pay per year of service or 55 percent of the final year's salary. This basic benefit is augmented by ITHP pension for service in excess of twenty-five years.

Finally, there is a plan requiring no minimum service, but retirement at age 55 or later. This is an alternative plan for teachers, nonuniformed employees, nonpedagogical employees of the board of education, and transit workers who are unlikely to meet the minimum service requirements of the second and third plans above. The plan provides for 1.53 percent of pay per year for each year of service plus an annuity from the employee's contribution plus pension from RITHP. Thus an employee who is 55 or older and who has worked for twenty-five years is entitled to a basic retirement allowance of 38.25 percent (1.53 x 25) of his preretirement salary plus an annuity from his own contribution to RITHP.

A word or two is in order regarding the normal service retirement allowance(s). The benefits reported above are comparatively new, dating from the mid-1960s. Some of the changes from the previous arrangements are:

First, until 1963, the city did not contribute toward RITHP for police and fire department employees. In that year, these employees were granted the ITHP coverage. Initially, the city contributed 2.5 percent of pay on their behalf, but in 1968 the rate was increased to 5 percent, retroactive to January 1, 1967, thus giving refunds to employees of 2.5 percent of their pay for eighteen months of pay.

Similarly, until 1970 the city contributed 2.5 percent of the sanitation workers' pay to RITHP, but since then this rate has been 5 percent. The same is true of the teachers: beginning in 1970 the city contributed 5 percent of teachers' pay toward RITHP, whereas this rate was 2.5 percent before that time.

The twenty or twenty-five years' service requirement is also of recent origin. For example, the teachers originally could retire at age 65 or after thirty-five years of service. Beginning in 1959, however, a teacher could retire at age 55 or after thirty years of service. In 1964 a new plan was introduced that provided retirement at age 55 with twenty-five years of service. This plan was further liberalized in 1970 when the teachers were given the option of retiring after twenty years' service but with benefits deferred until age 55, or retiring at age 55 with increased pension benefits. Similarly, NYCERS originally had three plans. Assuming an employee joined city employment at age 25, he or she could retire at age 58 (laborers and unskilled workers), at age 59 (mechanics and skilled workers), or at age 60 (clerical, administrative, professional, and technical workers). Presently, the employee can join the third or fourth plans discussed above.

Finally, the most important change was that the retirement benefits were related to the salary prevailing in the last year, or in some cases the salary just before retirement. Initially, the benefits were based on the average salary for five years before retirement including overtime pay. As a result of this liberalization, some employees were promoted just before retirement to give them the benefit of higher wages and salaries on which the retirement benefits would be computed.

Early Retirement Benefits: Vesting of Pension Rights. The provisions regarding retirement benefits before normal retirement age and service also differ from plan to plan. The career employees belonging to the NYCERS are fully vested after fifteen years of service, although the benefits cannot be collected before age 55. On the other hand, transit operating employees, also belonging to NYCERS, do not have vesting provisions. The policemen and firemen are fully vested after fifteen years of service and can claim the benefits at the age when twenty years of service has been completed. Teachers, like the career employees of NYCERS, can retire after fifteen years of service, although they cannot claim retirement benefits until they are 55 years old.

The benefit formula for early retirement also varies from system to system. For example, a TRS member under the twenty-year service plan gets 2.5 percent of final pay per year of service if he or she works for twenty years, but only 1.53 percent if he or she decides to retire after the minimum service of fifteen years. In both cases, however, the retiree gets annuities from his own and the city's contribution to the RITHP. On the other hand, policemen and firemen get 2.5 percent of final pay per year of service in basic benefit whether they retire after the normal service period (twenty years) or after fifteen years of service, the minimum for vesting.

Disability Benefits

The provisions of the present law governing disability benefits in New York City (and New York State) make a distinction between "ordinary" or non-service-connected disability and "service-connected" or accidental disability. Unfortunately, this distinction disregards whether the disability is "total" or "partial." It is quite possible that a service-connected disability is partial, whereas an ordinary disability is total: for example, an employee may develop a serious heart ailment while vacationing and not be able to return to work at all. The disability benefit provisions currently existing can be summarized as follows.

Ordinary Disability Benefits. The eligibility requirements as well as the benefit formulas vary considerably among the five actuarial pension systems. To qualify for the ordinary disability benefits, the career and transit employees of the NYCERS and the teachers must have a minimum service of ten years. If this condition is satisfied and if ordinary disability occurs, an employee gets 1.53 percent of final year's salary per year of service. In addition, the career employees of the NYCERS (but not the transit workers) and the teachers get annuities from their own and the city's contribution to the RITHP. On the other hand, there is no minimum service requirement for transit and housing police, police, uniformed correction officers, and firemen. They receive 33.33 percent of final annual pay for ten or fewer years of service, 50 percent of final pay for service between ten and twenty years, and 50 percent plus 2.5 percent of final pay for each year of service in excess of twenty years.

Service-Connected or Accidental Disability Benefits. Regardless of the years of service, all five pension systems provide an annual pension equal to 75 percent of the highest five-year average salary (career employees and transit workers of NYCERS and teachers) or 75 percent of the final annual salary (sanitation, transit and housing police, police, correction officers, and firemen), plus annuities from member contributions and the city's contribution to the RITHP. The sanitation workers, transit and housing police, police, correction officers, and firemen get an additional benefit in case the disability occurs after twenty years of service. The rate is 1.5 percent of average salary for each year in excess of twenty for sanitation workers and 1.67 percent for the other categories.

In cases of accidental disability, the benefits of some employees are to a certain extent offset by Workmen's Compensation received under the state and federal laws. Policemen, firemen, and teachers in New York City are exempted from this offset. Accidental benefits are exempt from federal income tax for the first $100 a week up to the "normal retirement age." Benefits received under the Workmen's Compensation laws are totally tax-exempt.

Social Security Disability Benefits. The disability benefits discussed above are in addition to the disability benefits provided under the social security system, which can be substantial.[3]

Social security pays the full primary insurance amount (PIA) to a disabled worker starting (under the 1972 amendments to the Social Security Act) with the fifth month of disability. The PIA typically provides a disabled employee with benefits ranging between 28 percent and 40 percent, averaging about 35 percent, of his final average salary at the social security wage base ($15,300 in 1976 and $16,500 in 1977). The social security disability family benefits provide a worker who is married and has one or more children with a benefit of up to approximately 61 percent of average earnings at the social security wage base, the percentage being higher for an employee whose final average salary is below the social security wage base. These figures are subject to the cost of living escalation provision effected by the 1972 amendments to the Social Security Act.

If the disability benefits provided by the city pension systems are added to those provided by social security, it is possible for the total benefit to exceed 100 percent of the net (after-tax) preretirement income of some beneficiaries. For example, in the case of accidental disability, most city pension plans provide 75 percent of the final (average) salary in annual disability benefits, and the social security disability benefits average to about 35 percent of the final salary. Together, these benefits amount to 110 percent of the final salary. Since most accidental disability benefits are tax-exempt at the local,

---

[3] For details, see U.S. Department of Health, Education, and Welfare, Social Security Administration, *Social Security Handbook*, February 1974, p. 97.

state, and federal (up to $5,200 per year) levels, the effective benefit amounts to about 138 percent of the final net salary of the beneficiary.

Death Benefits

The city pension systems provide two types of death benefits: accidental or service-connected and "ordinary." Neither takes into account the social security survivors' benefits, such as benefits to widows, widowers, children, mothers, and so on.

Accidental Death Benefits. The eligibility requirements and the benefit formulas are more or less uniform for all the five actuarial pension systems. There is no minimum service requirement. Generally, a pension equal to 50 percent of highest five-year average salary is paid to the widow or child(ren) under 18 or dependent parent(s). The beneficiary also gets the member's and the city's contribution to the RITHP.

Ordinary Death Benefits. These are of two types: benefits for death while in active service and those for death after normal retirement service. In case an employee dies while in service but before completing the minimum service requirement, his beneficiary gets a lump sum about equal to a multiple of his salary plus the money he has contributed to the pension fund and the city's contribution to RITHP. The lump sum paid depends upon the length of service. Generally, all employees are entitled to the last six months' salary for less than ten years' service and to the last twelve months' salary for ten or more years of service. Career employees of NYCERS, teachers belonging to TRS, and the employees of the board of education get twice the last twelve months' salary if they have worked for twenty or more years.

Until 1961 a very peculiar practice prevailed regarding death benefits of a member who died while still in active service although eligible for retirement. If such a death occurred, the beneficiary could get only a year's or at most two years' final salary plus the member's and the city's contributions to the RITHP. If this member had retired, the beneficiary would have been entitled to the full actuarial value of his or her death benefits (discussed below). This was called the "death gamble." Since 1965 the death gamble no longer exists. If an employee dies while in active service but after being eligible for retirement, his or her beneficiary is entitled to full pension and annuity reserves.

Death benefits after retirement are based on the retiree's choice of benefit option. Just prior to retirement, the retiree may choose any one of the following plans:

- *Option 1: return of reserve.* Upon the death of the retiree, the beneficiary is paid a lump sum equal to any excess of the actuarial reserve established at retirement over the total of benefit payments already made.
- *Option 2: 100 percent joint-and-survivor.* Upon the retiree's death, the amount of the adjusted benefit is continued for the life of the beneficiary.
- *Option 3: 50 percent joint-and-survivor.* Upon the death of the retired member, one-half of the adjusted benefit is continued for the life of the beneficiary.
- *Option 4: any other.* Other options include a lump sum upon death, provided that, with the appropriate reduction in the member's own monthly benefit, the total has the same actuarial value as the original retirement allowance.

Special Benefits

In addition to service retirement allowances, disability benefits, and death benefits, the city pays some special benefits to selected groups of employees.

Union Annuity Funds. Since 1966, pursuant to collective bargaining agreements, the city has been contributing per diem amounts toward the purchase of annuities payable upon retirement to certain groups of employees. These amounts are paid directly to the unions (the TRS receives them on behalf of the teachers) or to associations of employees (such as the firefighters' association) distinct from their union. The per diem rate of contribution and the employees covered for the year 1976 are given in Table 27.

There is some question as to the legality of these contributions. The New York State comptroller maintains that they are in violation of Section 113(a) of the New York State Retirement and Social Security Law, which states that, "No municipality, after April twelfth, nineteen hundred twenty-two, shall create any retirement system for its officers or employees."[4] Since the union annuity funds are in effect pension funds, and since they were established only recently, the state comptroller is probably right in this matter.

Despite the law, the contributions to union annuity funds continue. In February 1976 the New York Public Interest Research Group

---

[4] Office of the Comptroller, State of New York, *Audit Report on Survey of Various Fringe Benefit Plans Granted to Employee Associations by the City of New York*, Report no. NYC–3.73.

TABLE 27

New York City Contributions to Union Annuity Funds, Fiscal Year 1976

Employee Group	Per Diem Cost (dollars)	Approximate Number of Employees	Approximate Cost (millions of dollars)
Firefighters	1.00	10,300	2.69
Fire officers	to 2.65	1,700	1.18
Patrolmen	1.00	23,000	6.00
Police officers	to 2.65	5,000	3.46
Housing police	1.00	900	0.23
Officers	to 2.65	200	0.14
Transit police	1.00	2,970	0.78
Officers	to 2.65	400	0.28
Corrections officers	1.00	3,000	0.78
Officers	to 2.65	300	0.21
Sanitation workers	1.00	9,500	2.48
Officers	to 2.65	1,500	1.04
Teachers[a]	400 per year	N.A.	11.60
Supervisors	550 per year	N.A.	—
Transit employees	500 per year	10,000	5.50
Total	—	—	35.90

[a] At the maximum salary step only.

Source: Temporary Commission on City Finances, *The Fiscal Impact of Retirement Benefits: Some Proposals for Reform*, Sixth Interim Report to the Mayor, May 1976, Table X, p. 24.

and four New York City taxpayers filed a suit in the State Supreme Court (New York County) challenging the payments. The suit asks for the stoppage of these contributions as well as for the return of all money (with interest) paid to employee associations or unions (minus the benefits already paid the retirees). As yet, the suit has not been resolved.

Heart Bill. The heart bill, enacted by the New York state legislature on a year-to-year basis, applies to police and fire department pension funds. The bill states that *any* heart disease suffered by policemen and firemen is presumed to be service-connected and entitles the affected person to accidental disability pension equal to 75 percent of final pay. Ordinary retirement entitles a policeman or fireman to only 50 percent of final salary.

TABLE 28

COMPARISON OF ACTUAL AND EXPECTED SEPARATION FROM ACTIVE SERVICE, JUNE 30, 1969, TO JUNE 30, 1974, NEW YORK CITY FIRE DEPARTMENT PENSION FUND, ARTICLE 1–B

Type of Retirement	Actual	Expected	Actual ÷ Expected
Service	486	1,542.7	0.32
Ordinary disability	267	240.0	1.11
Accidental	749	30.5	24.56

SOURCE: Temporary Commission on City Finances, *The Fiscal Impact of Retirement Benefits: Some Proposals for Reform*, Sixth Interim Report to the Mayor, May 1976, Table IX, p. 22.

There seems to be little doubt that policemen and firemen have taken advantage of the bill, as Table 28 reveals.

Special Features of Public Retirement Systems in New York State

The following features of the public employee retirement systems in New York State may be noted.

Constitutional Guarantee of Pension Benefits. Article V, Section 7 of the New York State Constitution provides that once a permanent pension or retirement benefit has been granted a member of the public retirement system (state, city, or local), it cannot subsequently be reduced, impaired, or discontinued. Thus, policemen and firemen who are already employed can retire after twenty years of service at half pay regardless of age, even though the city's fiscal plight is such that it cannot afford to continue this generous pension plan. Any changes made in pensions are applicable only to employees who are appointed after the changes.

Incidentally, the constitutional guarantee does not extend to the ITHP benefits or to those under the heart bill, for they are enacted on an annual basis by the state legislature and can be changed at any time. As noted previously, beginning in January 1976 the city's rates of contributions to ITHP were halved.

Tax Treatment of Pension Benefits. Article XVI, Section 5 of the New York State Constitution provides that the pensions paid by the City of New York (and other municipalities in the state) are exempt from city and state income taxes, although the part of the pension that is provided by the city's contribution is subject to federal income tax.

It is interesting to observe that retirees under private pension plans are not exempt from city and state income taxes. Therefore, the after-tax income of such retirees is less than that of public employees, assuming that other factors remain the same.